the vegetarian book

charmaine solomon

HAMLYN

First published in Great Britain
in 1997 by Hamlyn,
an imprint of Reed International Books
Limited Michelin House, 81 Fulham Road
London SW3 6RB
and Auckland, Melbourne, Singapore and
Toronto

Published 1996 by Mandarin
a part of Reed Books Australia
35 Cotham Road, Kew, Victoria 3101
a division of Reed International Books
Australia Pty Limited

First published in 1993 by Hamlyn Australia
as part of Charmaine Solomon's Asian
Cooking Library.

Copyright text © Charmaine Solomon 1993
Copyright photographs © Michael Cook 1993

All rights reserved. Without limiting the
rights under copyright above, no part of this
publication may be reproduced, stored in or
introduced into a retrieval system, or
transmitted in any form or by any means
(electronic, mechanical, photocopying,
recording or otherwise), without the prior
written permission of both the copyright
owner and the publisher.

ISBN for UK edition 0 600 59316 9
A CIP catalogue for this book is available
from the British Library

Solomon, Charmaine.
 The vegetarian book.
 Includes index.
 ISBN for Australian edition 1 86330 444 4.
 1. Vegetarian cookery. 2. Cookery
 (Seafood). 3. Cookery, Oriental. I. Title.

641.5636

Designed by Guy Mirabella
Photographs by Rodney Weidland,
Michael Cook, Reg Morrison
Styling by Margaret Alcock
Food cooked by Nina Harris, Jill Pavey
China: Villeroy & Boch, Australia Pty Ltd
Typeset in Times and Univers by
J&M Typesetting
Produced by Mandarin Offset
Printed and bound in Hong Kong

A Metric/Imperial guide to Australian solid and liquid measures

Liquid Measures

Australian	Metric	Imperial
1 cup	250 ml	8 fl oz
1/2 cup	125 ml	4 fl oz
1/3 cup	75 ml	3 fl oz

Solid Measures

Australian	Metric	Imperial
1 cup	300 g	10 oz
1/2 cup	150 g	5 oz
1/3 cup	125 g	4 oz

Liquid Measures/Teaspoons/Tablespoons
A teaspoon holds approximately 5 ml in both Australia and Britain. The British standard tablespoon holds 15 ml, whilst the Australian holds 20 ml.

Australian	British
1 teaspoon	1 teaspoon
1 tablespoon	1 tablespoon
2 tablespoons	2 tablespoons
3 1/2 tablespoons	3 tablespoons
4 tablespoons	3 1/2 tablespoons

Notes
Convert cup measures to metric or imperial measures where necessary. Use one set of measurements only and not a mixture. Standard level spoon measurements are used in all recipes.
Eggs should be full fat unless otherwise stated.
Milk should be full fat unless otherwise stated.
Pepper should be freshly milled unless otherwise stated.
Fresh herbs should be used unless otherwise stated. If unavailable use dried herbs as an alternative but halve the quantities stated.

For ease of reference:
Capsicum = Pepper
Eggplant = Aubergine
Zucchini = Courgette

dry-fried okra

Okra is not very well known in western countries, but is one of the most popular vegetables in Asia and the Middle East. Originating in Africa, it was taken to the New World and is widely used in Creole cookery. When buying okra, it is important to choose small, tender beans rather than large, well seasoned ones. The test is to bend the thin tip – if fresh and tender it will snap clean off, but if old and tough it will bend. Its main characteristic is a mucilaginous quality much prized as a thickener in gumbos and curries.

serves 6

- 750 g (1½ lb) small, tender okra
- 2 tablespoons oil
- 1 teaspoon black mustard seeds
- 2 sprigs fresh curry leaves
- 1 onion, finely chopped
- 2 teaspoons finely chopped fresh ginger
- 2 teaspoons ground coriander
- 1 teaspoon ground cumin
- 1 teaspoon ground turmeric
- salt to taste
- 1 teaspoon Garam Masala (see p. 00)
- lemon juice to taste

Wash and dry okra and cut across into thick slices. Heat oil in a wok or frying pan and fry mustard seeds and curry leaves until seeds pop. (Cover the pan or seeds will jump all over the stove.) Add onion and ginger, stir-fry until soft and golden. Add ground spices and stir over heat for a minute longer.

Add okra, toss and fry until coated with spices, then cover and cook for 3 to 4 minutes until okra is tender but still crisp. Sprinkle with salt, Garam Masala and lemon juice and serve with rice.

Eggplants, pumpkins, zucchini, tomatoes, capsicums, cucumbers, ridged gourds and bitter melons are only some of the 'fruit vegetables' that are so plentiful, colourful and downright delicious. Eggplant is one of the most flavoursome of vegetables and is a mainstay of Asian vegetarian cookery. Fruits like tomatoes, capsicums and cucumbers may be used raw or cooked, giving such different results but delicious either way.

stuffed and braised banana chillies

The larger the chilli, the milder and sweeter it is, so when you choose banana chillies or Hungarian sweet peppers, they aren't going to burn your socks off!

serves 6

- 12 banana chillies or Hungarian sweet peppers
- 750 g (1½ lb) potatoes
- 3 tablespoons ghee
- 3 tablespoons oil
- 2 onions, finely chopped
- 2 tablespoons chopped fresh dill or mint
- 1½ teaspoons salt or to taste
- freshly ground black pepper to taste
- 4–6 fresh hot chillies, seeded and chopped
- 2 teaspoons finely grated fresh ginger
- 1 teaspoon turmeric
- 1½ teaspoons cumin seeds, roasted and crushed
- 3 large ripe tomatoes, peeled, seeded and chopped or 360 g (12 oz) canned tomatoes
- 1 teaspoon Garam Masala (see p. 4)
- 3 tablespoons chopped fresh coriander

Wash and dry chillies, slit one side from just below stem and remove seeds and membranes. Prepare filling by boiling potatoes until tender, peeling and mashing them.

Heat half the ghee and oil in a heavy saucepan and cook onions over medium low heat, stirring frequently, until soft and turning golden. Remove half the onions to a bowl and mix in dill or mint, salt, pepper and half the hot chillies. Combine thoroughly with potatoes, tasting and adjusting seasonings so mixture is well flavoured. Stuff banana chillies with this mixture.

Heat remaining ghee and oil in a frying pan and fry chillies until they blister slightly. Reheat cooked onions in saucepan with ginger and remaining hot chillies, turmeric and cumin. Stir-fry for a few minutes until fragrant. Add tomatoes and Garam Masala, cover and simmer until tomatoes are pulpy. Season with salt to taste. Lay chillies in a single layer in sauce and simmer for 5 minutes. Sprinkle with coriander and serve with rice or chapatis.

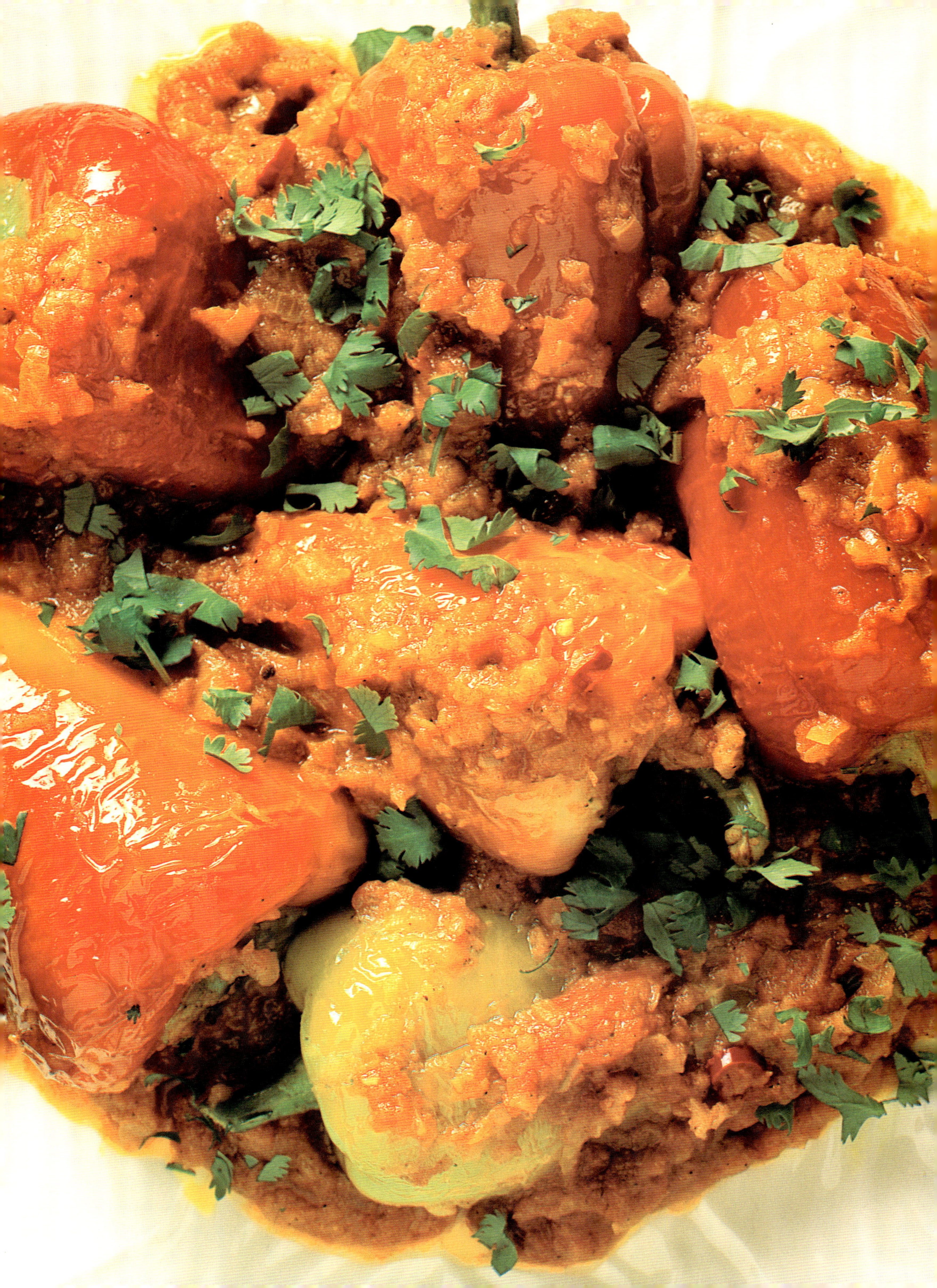

cucumber
or ridged gourd curry

Sometimes it is possible to find the tender, sweet gourds that make mild and delicious coconut curries. When they are scarce, use cucumbers.

serves 4

- 1 or 2 ridged gourds (about 240 g or 8 oz) or 4 seedless cucumbers
- 2 tablespoons oil
- 1 onion, finely sliced
- 2 sprigs fresh curry leaves
- 3 fresh green chillies
- 2 cloves garlic, sliced
- 6 slices fresh ginger
- 1 small cinnamon stick
- 1 stem lemon grass, bruised or 3 strips lemon rind
- 1 teaspoon turmeric
- 360 ml (12 fl oz) canned coconut milk
- 1 teaspoon salt or to taste

Wash gourds and with a vegetable peeler remove sharp ridges. Cut into slices, about 2.5 cm (1 in) thick. Heat oil in a saucepan and gently fry onion, curry leaves, whole chillies, garlic, ginger and cinnamon until onion is soft. Add lemon grass or rind, turmeric and coconut milk. If coconut milk is thick, mix with an equal quantity of water and if thin and watery use only half as much water or none at all, but liquid should total about 720 ml (24 fl oz). Simmer, uncovered, about 10 minutes then add gourd and continue to cook uncovered until vegetable is tender but still holding its shape. Season to taste. Serve with rice.

Variations

Instead of the gourds or cucumbers, you can make this recipe using dark green zucchinis and untoasted cashew nuts. You should soak the cashews in hot water for at least 30 minutes.

Snake gourd – deep green and a metre or more in length – is cooked in the same way. Peel thinly or scrape the skin (as for carrots), cut in thick slices and scoop out seeds, then proceed as above.

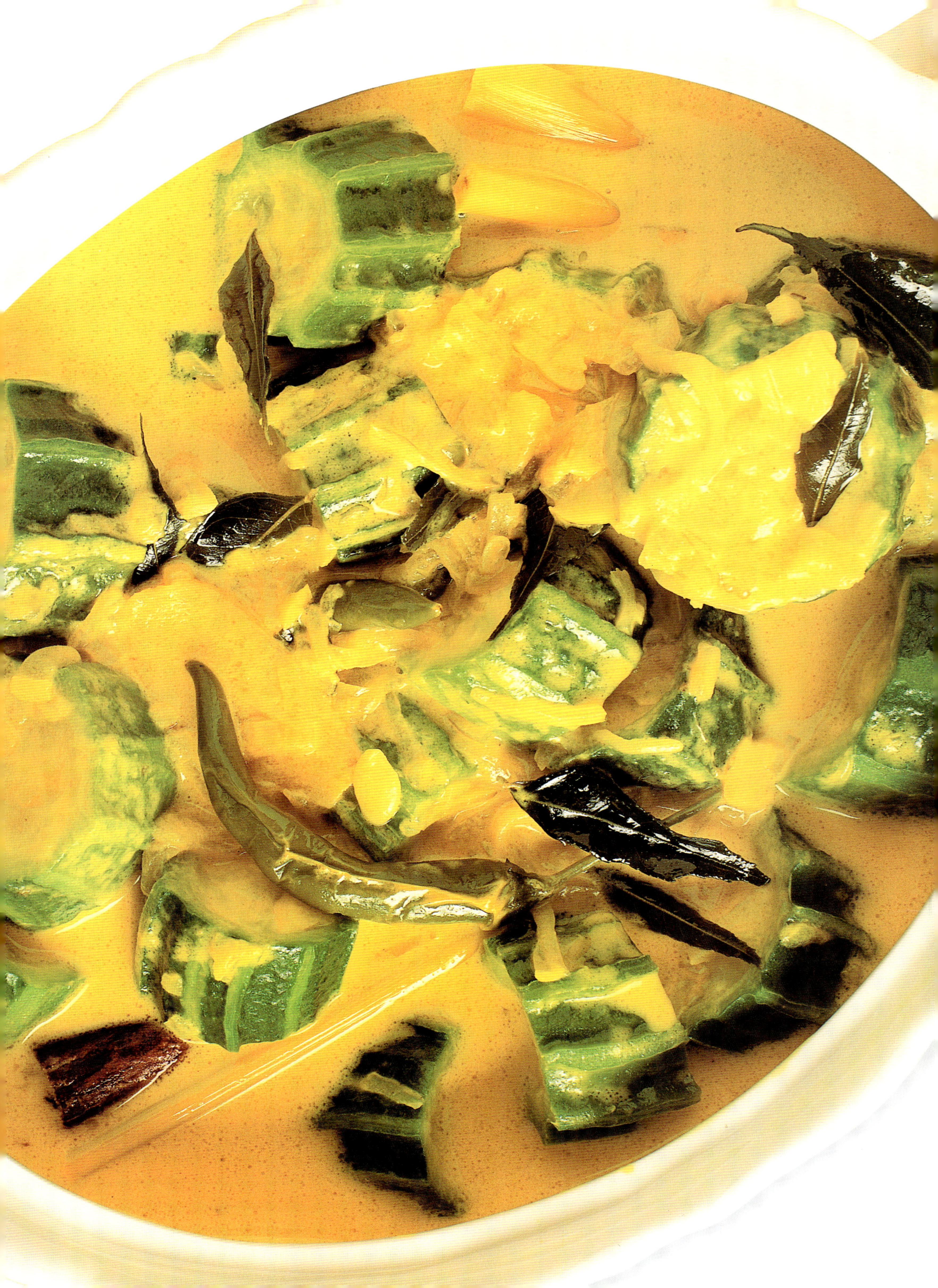

chinese -style eggplant

This vegetarian dish rivals fish, flesh or fowl in tastiness.

serves 4

- 750 g (1½ lb) eggplant
- peanut oil for deep-frying
- 2 teaspoons finely chopped fresh ginger
- 2 teaspoons crushed garlic
- 60 ml (2 fl oz) dry sherry
- 60 ml (2 fl oz) soy sauce
- 1 tablespoon vinegar
- 2 tablespoons sugar
- 2 teaspoons oriental sesame oil
- 1 teaspoon chilli bean sauce

Wash and dry eggplants and slice thickly. Heat oil and fry eggplant in batches until golden brown. Drain on paper towels. Pour oil into a metal bowl and return a tablespoon of oil to wok. On gentle heat fry ginger and garlic, stirring until golden. Add remaining ingredients and stir until sugar dissolves. Return eggplant and cook uncovered, turning eggplant until sauce is syrupy and almost absorbed. Serve with steamed rice.

Note If cooking in an iron wok, transfer to a dish immediately it is ready, or the acid in the dish can cause a metallic taste.

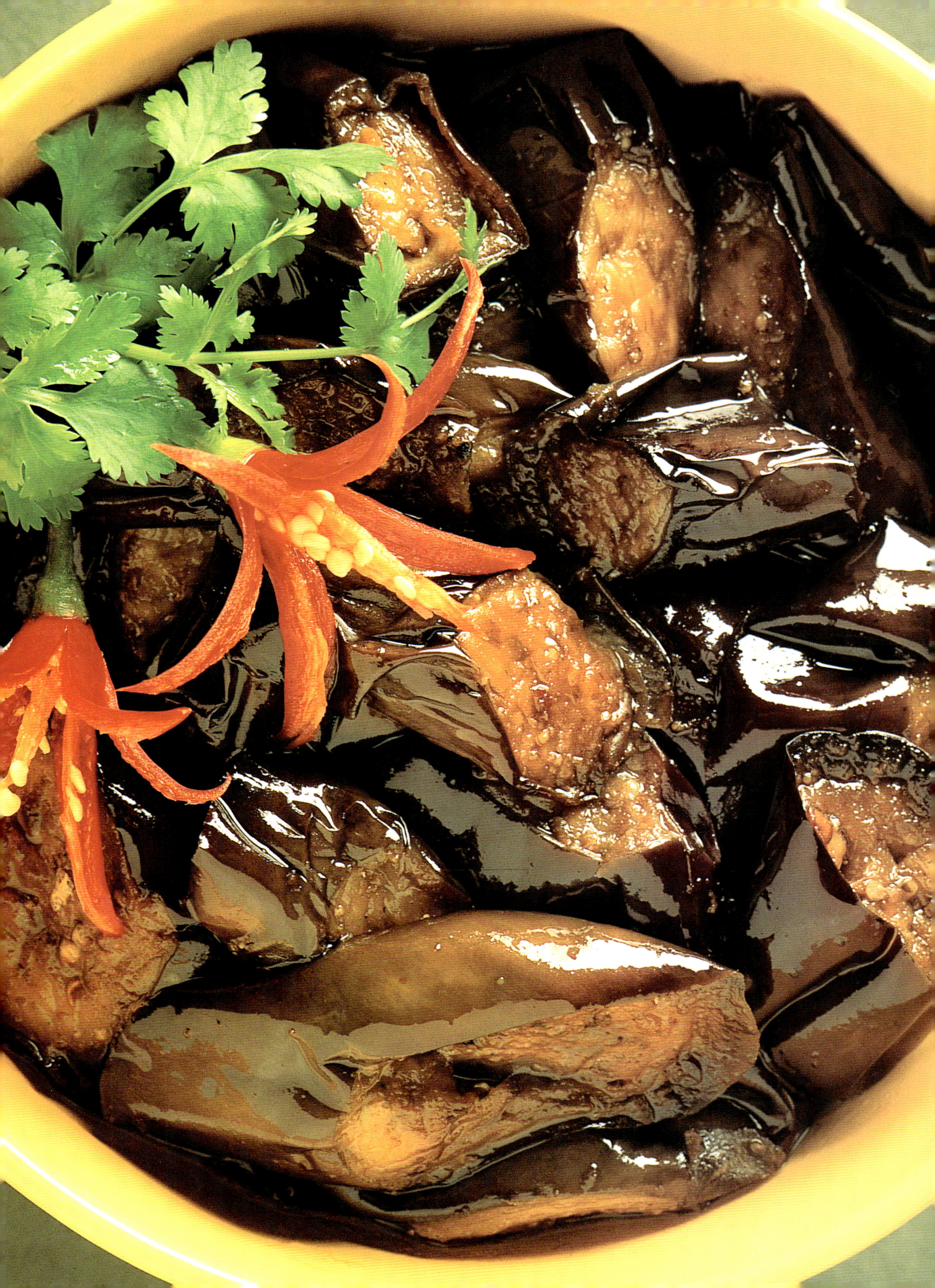

creamy eggplant relish

serves 4

500 g (1 lb) eggplant
½ teaspoon salt
1 teaspoon ground turmeric
90 g (3 oz) raw peanuts
1 small red capsicum, diced
peanut oil for deep frying

120 ml (4 oz) thick sour cream
240 ml (8 oz) thick natural yoghurt
1 clove garlic
½ teaspoon sea salt
1 teaspoon finely grated fresh ginger
2 fresh chillies, optional

Wash and dry eggplant, cut into wedges and rub with salt and half the turmeric. Leave 20 minutes, then blot on paper towels.

Heat 60 ml (2 fl oz) oil and fry peanuts until golden. Drain. Stir-fry diced capsicum and remove. Pour in oil for deep frying and fry eggplant on high heat until golden brown outside and soft inside. Drain on paper towels. Combine sour cream, yoghurt, garlic crushed to a smooth purée with salt, remaining turmeric and fresh ginger. Spoon sauce on serving plate, arrange capsicum in centre and eggplant around. Garnish with peanuts and slices of chilli.

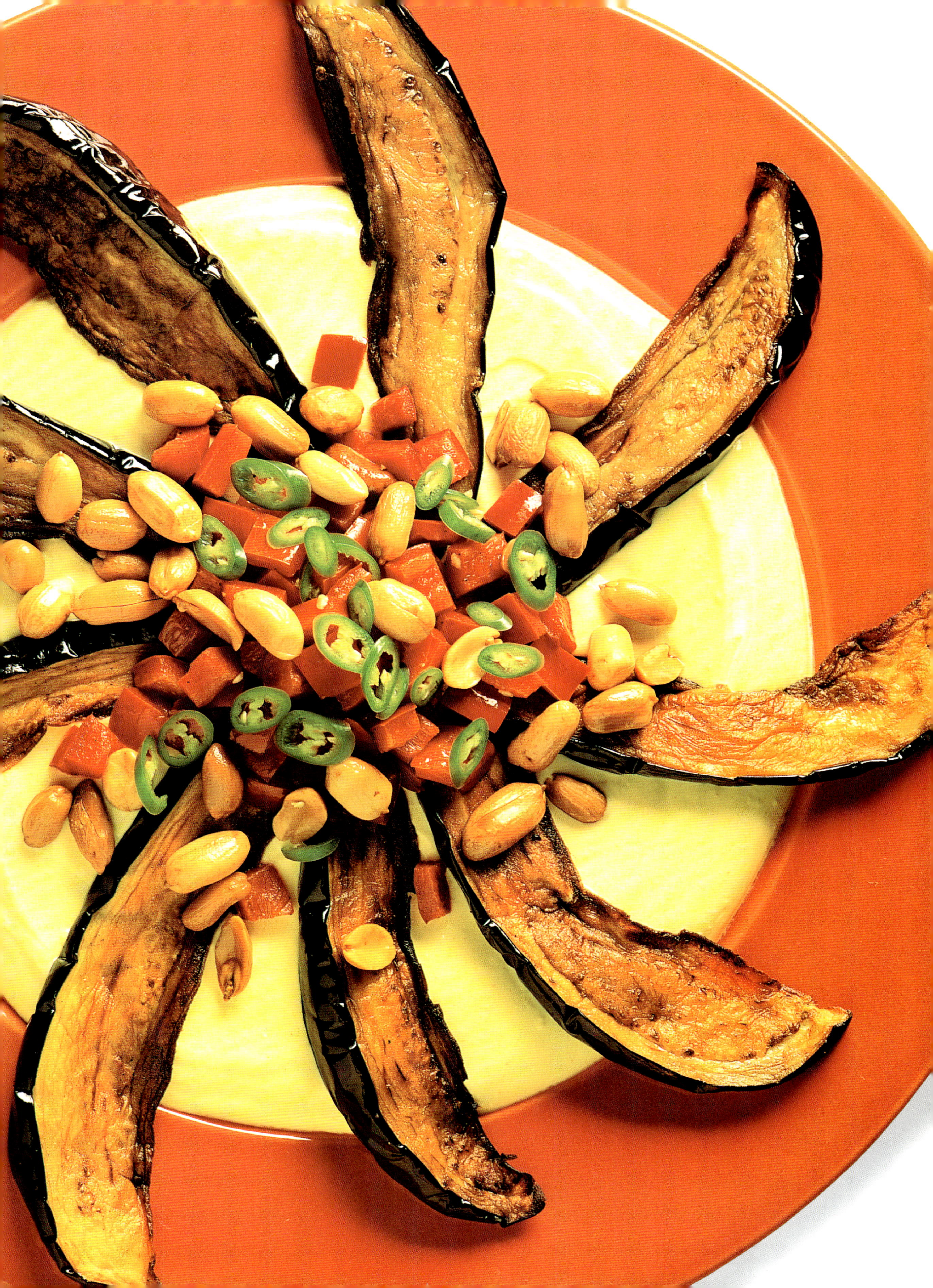

zucchini or squash dry-fry

When a vegetable has as much water content as zucchini or squash, it needs to be degorged before cooking if the flavour is not to be swamped by the amount of liquid it will exude. The time spent doing this is well worth the final result.

serves 4

500 g (1 lb) zucchini or squash
salt
2 tablespoons ghee or oil
1 teaspoon cumin seed
½ teaspoon kalonji (nigella) seeds

1 onion, finely chopped
1 or 2 fresh red chillies, seeded and sliced
120 ml (4 oz) thick yoghurt

Grate the zucchini coarsely into a large bowl. Sprinkle with 1 teaspoon salt, mix well and set aside for 30 minutes. Squeeze out all the liquid with both hands. (This may be saved for a soup or vegetable gravy.)

Heat ghee in a wok or frying pan and fry cumin and kalonji until fragrant and cumin turns brown. Add onion and chillies and cook until onion is soft and golden. Mix in grated zucchini and stir over medium high heat until almost all liquid evaporates. Serve as is, or stir into yoghurt.

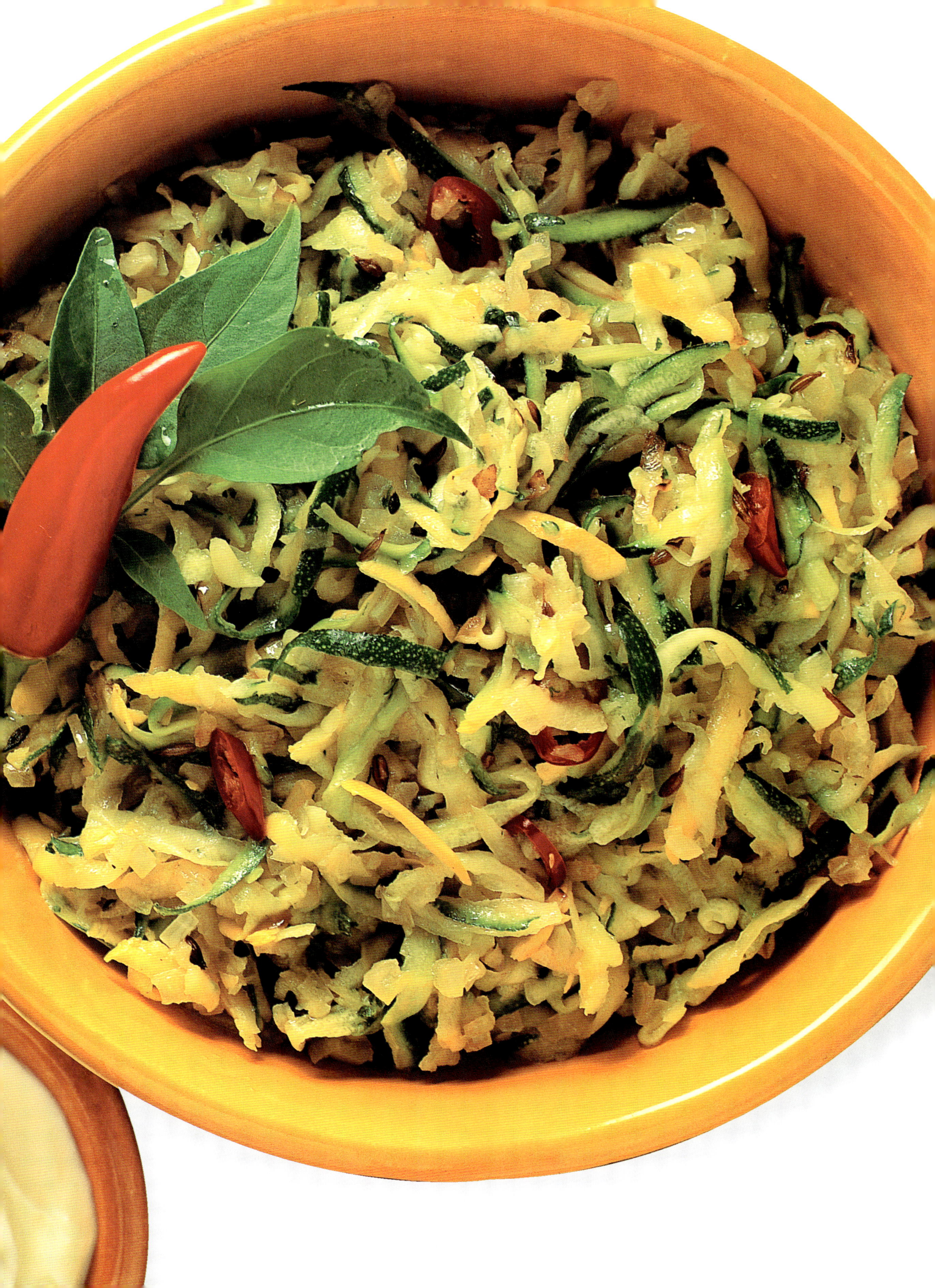

pineapple curry

serves 6 to 8

- 1 slightly under-ripe pineapple
- 2 onions, roughly chopped
- 4 cloves garlic, peeled
- 3 or 4 fresh red chillies, seeded
- 1 teaspoon shrimp paste
- 2 teaspoons Fragrant Ground Spices (see below)
- 2 tablespoons oil
- 240 ml (8 fl oz) canned coconut milk
- 1 teaspoon salt or to taste
- 2 teaspoons palm sugar or brown sugar
- 20 fresh basil leaves

Using a sharp stainless steel knife remove pineapple skin. With a series of diagonal cuts forming a V, remove 'eyes' three at a time. Cut pineapple in long wedges, remove core. Purée onions, garlic, chillies, shrimp paste and spices in blender. Heat oil and fry purée on low heat for 15 minutes, stirring. Add pineapple, coconut milk, salt and sugar. Stir and simmer for 5 minutes. Sprinkle with basil leaves and serve as an extra dish with rice and curries.

fragrant ground spices

- 1 teaspoon ground cardamom
- ½ teaspoon ground cinnamon
- ½ teaspoon ground nutmeg
- ¼ teaspoon ground cloves

While there are many different components that give delightful complexity and depth to the flavours of a dish, only a tiny amount of each is required. I suggest making spice mixes to avoid the tedium of measuring many small quantities for each recipe. It is much better to make up, for instance, four times the quantity and store it in an airtight jar. Label each mixture clearly and store it out of the sunlight. The freezer is the best place for keeping spices at optimum freshness. To ensure even distribution, shake or stir before measuring out the amount required.

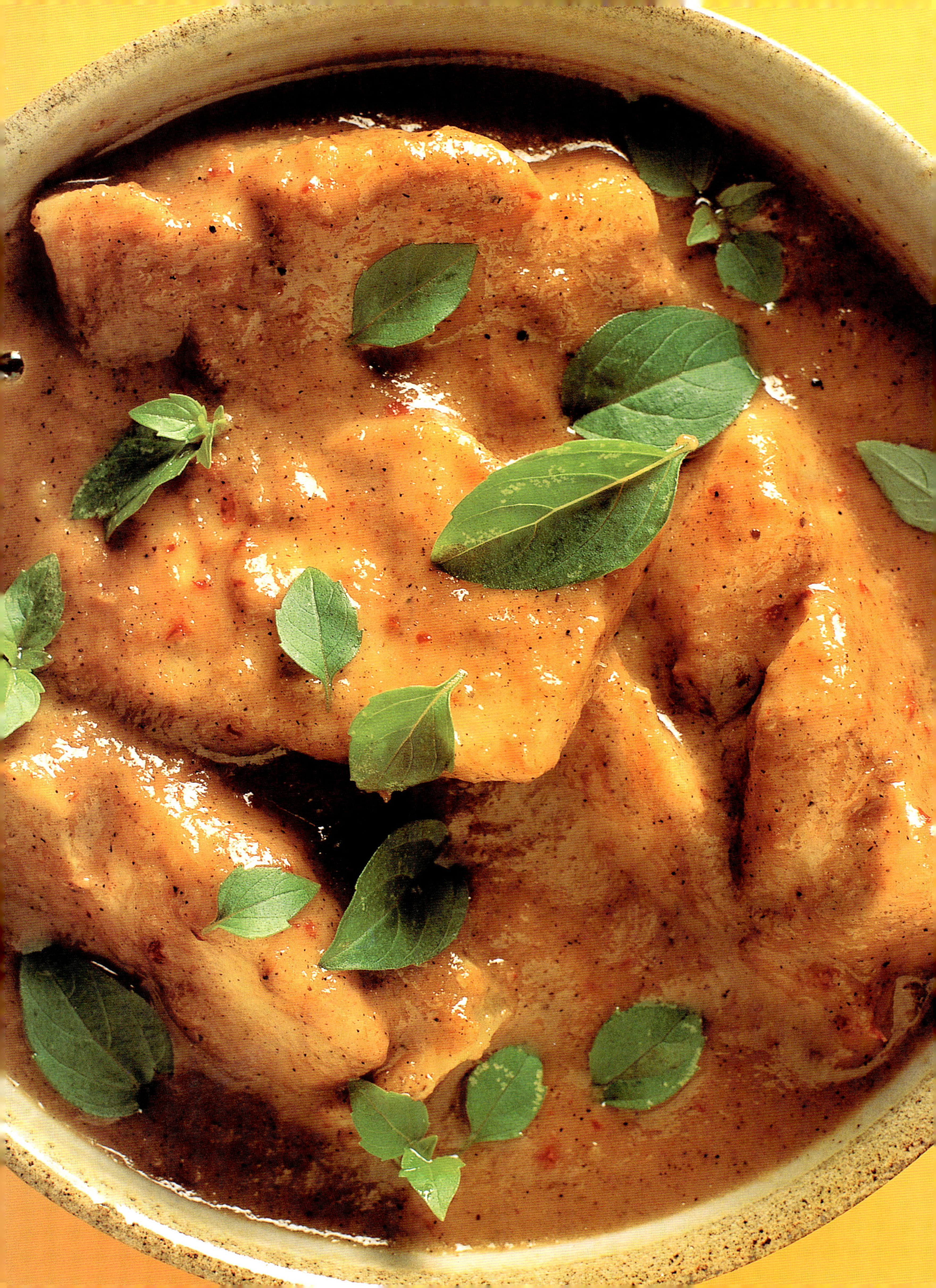

pumpkin in coconut milk

serves 6

750 g (1½ lb) yellow pumpkin
240 ml (8 fl oz) canned coconut milk
2 onions, sliced finely
3 cloves garlic, sliced
5 cm (2 in) cinnamon stick

2 sprigs fresh curry leaves
3 fresh chillies, split lengthways
1 teaspoon turmeric
1 teaspoon salt or to taste

Peel and seed pumpkin and cut into cubes. In a large saucepan put coconut milk with an equal amount of water, add all ingredients except pumpkin and stir while bringing to the boil over medium heat. Reduce heat and simmer, uncovered, for 10 minutes before adding pumpkin. Cover and simmer until tender. Serve with rice and accompaniments.

Leafy vegetables are the ones most of us had to be coerced into eating in our youth. If the truth be told, some secretly resist them even into maturity; but when introduced to the same despised greens properly prepared, even the most reluctant develop a liking for spinach, cabbage, broccoli and others.

When purchasing green vegetables, be especially watchful that they are fresh, crisp, firm and not yellowed or withered in any way. These vegetables are particularly good cooked in coconut milk with spices.

Asian market gardeners are providing us with an amazing choice of what is lumped together under the name 'Chinese cabbage'. Try to get to know these vegetables by the names they are sold under and find out just how flavoursome are gai choy (mustard cabbage), gai larn (Chinese broccoli), Shanghai bok choy (miniature chard) and choy sum (Chinese flowering cabbage), to name just a few.

broccoli with peanut sauce

serves 4 to 6

- 360 g (12 oz) broccoli
- 2 tablespoons peanut oil
- 1 tablespoon Pepper and Coriander Paste (see below)
- 120 ml (4 fl oz) canned coconut milk
- 1 teaspoon palm sugar or brown sugar
- ½ teaspoon salt
- 4 kaffir lime leaves, optional
- 2 tablespoons crunchy peanut butter
- 20 fresh basil leaves, preferably lemon basil

Blanch broccoli for 2 minutes in a little lightly salted boiling water, lift out broccoli and save cooking liquid.

Heat peanut oil and fry Pepper and Coriander Paste on medium low heat, stirring constantly until fragrant. Add coconut milk mixed with 120 ml (4 fl oz) cooking liquid and stir as it comes to a simmer. Stir in sugar, salt, lime leaves and broccoli, simmer for 5 minutes. Add peanut butter and dissolve in sauce, pressing with the back of a spoon to disperse. Stir in basil leaves and serve with rice.

pepper and coriander paste

makes about 1 cup

- 1 large bunch fresh coriander with roots
- 1 tablespoon whole black peppercorns
- 1 tablespoon chopped garlic
- 2 teaspoons salt
- 2 tablespoons lemon juice

Wash coriander thoroughly, scrubbing roots and separating stems to remove sand, which clings, then chop. Roast peppercorns in a dry pan for a minute or two until fragrant.

Put all ingredients in electric blender and blend to a smooth purée, adding a little water if necessary. If paste is made using mortar and pestle do not add lemon juice until after the pounding has resulted in a smooth paste.

cauliflower with green masala

serves 6

500 g (1 lb) cauliflower
2 tablespoons oil
1 teaspoon black mustard seeds
½ teaspoon cumin seeds
½ teaspoon kalonji (nigella) seeds

2 teaspoons Green Masala Paste (see below) or 1 teaspoon each grated garlic and ginger
1 teaspoon salt or to taste

Break cauliflower into florets, then slice each floret thickly, leaving a piece of stem on each. Heat oil in a wok or saucepan and fry mustard, kalonji and cumin seeds, stirring until mustard seeds pop. Add Green Masala Paste and cook, stirring, for 1 minute. Add cauliflower, toss with spice mixture, then pour in 60 ml (2 fl oz) water and immediately cover pan with lid and use steam to finish cooking cauliflower, it will take about 5 minutes. Season and serve with rice or chapatis.

green masala paste

makes about 2 cups

1 teaspoon fenugreek seeds
8 cloves garlic
2 tablespoons chopped fresh ginger
60 g (2 oz) fresh mint sprigs
1 small bunch fresh coriander
120 ml (4 fl oz) vinegar

3 teaspoons salt
2 teaspoons turmeric
1 teaspoon ground cardamom
½ teaspoon ground cloves
120 ml (4 fl oz) vegetable oil
120 ml (4 fl oz) oriental sesame oil

Soak fenugreek seeds in 60 ml (2 fl oz) water overnight. Combine with other ingredients except oil and blend on high speed until you have a smooth purée. Heat vegetable oil and when very hot add purée and stir until mixture boils, then turn off heat. Cool, stir in sesame oil and pour into a jar. Add more sesame oil if it does not completely cover the mixture. Use a clean dry spoon to remove paste. Add to stir-fried vegetables, stir into rice or add to curries for an extra boost of fresh herb flavour. You can store this paste for a few weeks in the refrigerator.

spinach with mixed vegetables

serves 4 to 6

- 1 bunch spinach
- 500 g (1 lb) pumpkin
- 240 g (8 oz) okra or snake beans
- 80 g (2½ oz) fresh shelled peas
- 2 tablespoons oil
- 1 teaspoon black mustard seeds
- 1 medium onion, finely chopped
- 1 teaspoon finely grated fresh ginger
- 1 clove garlic, finely chopped
- ½ teaspoon ground turmeric
- 90 g (3 oz) raw cashews, soaked 30 minutes

Discard tough stems from spinach, wash leaves well and chop roughly. Cut pumpkin into dice. Wash okra and trim stem ends. If using beans, trim and cut into short lengths.

Heat oil in a heavy saucepan and fry mustard seeds until they begin to pop. Add onion, ginger and garlic and fry, stirring occasionally, until onion is soft. Stir in turmeric and fry for 1 minute more. Add prepared vegetables, drained cashews and 240 ml (8 fl oz) hot water. Cover and simmer until vegetables are tender. Continue to cook uncovered, stirring frequently, until liquid reduces. Serve with rice or chapatis – if serving with the latter, let it cook to a drier consistency.

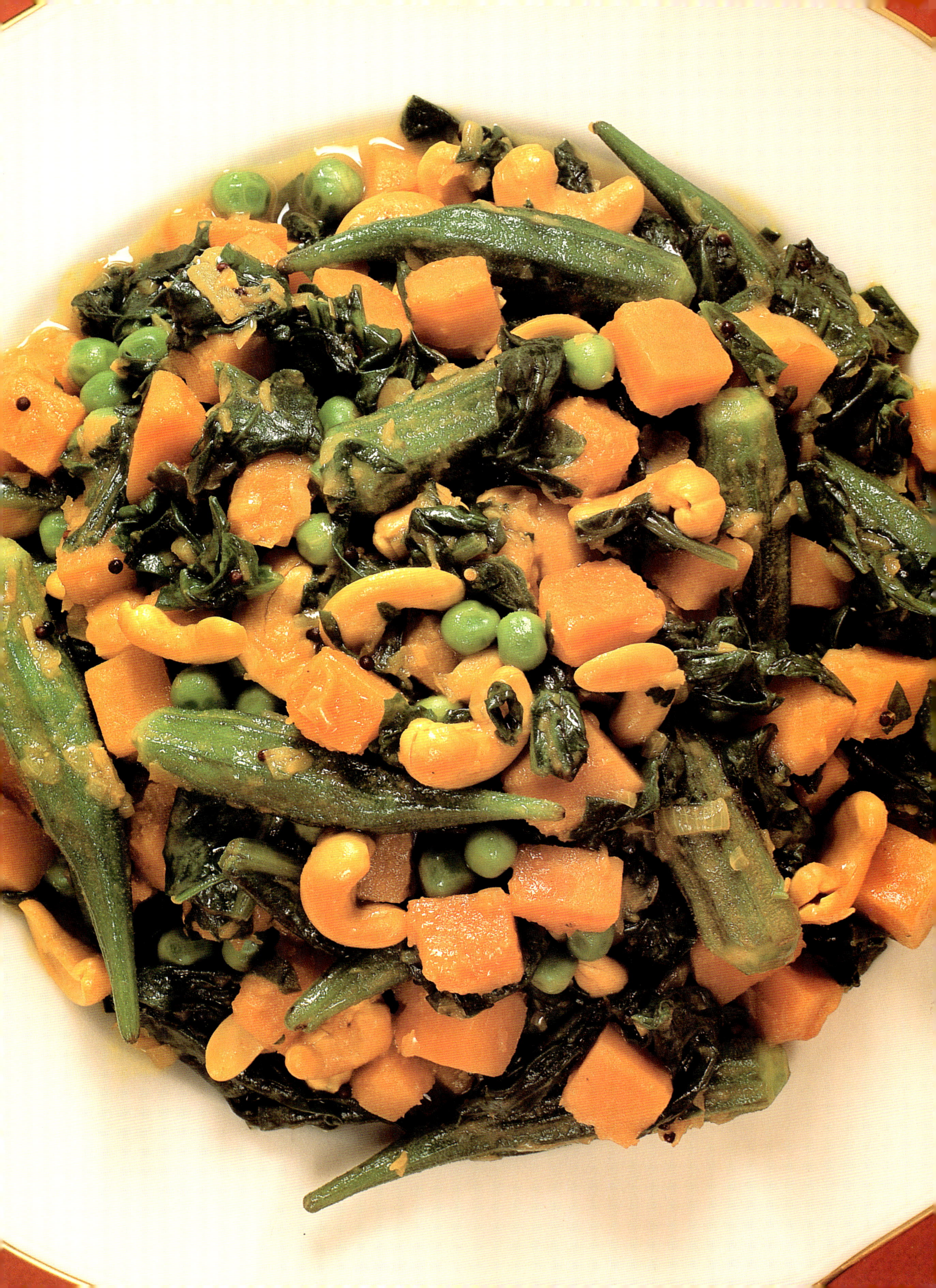

bok choy, braised

Bok choy is chard cabbage with white stems and dark green leaves.

serves 6

500 g (1 lb) bok choy
2 tablespoons peanut oil
6 thin slices fresh ginger
2 cloves garlic, finely chopped

2 tablespoons light soy sauce
1 teaspoon sugar
1 teaspoon oriental sesame oil

Wash bok choy well, separating leaves. Shake dry. Cut bok choy into bite-size lengths, discarding any tough leaves.

Heat a wok and add oil, swirling to coat cooking surface. Fry ginger slices for a few seconds, add garlic and fry gently until pale golden, then add bok choy and stir-fry vigorously for 1 minute. Pour in soy sauce mixed with sugar and 2 tablespoons water. Cover and steam for 2 minutes. Uncover and stir-fry once more over high heat until liquid has almost evaporated, then sprinkle sesame oil over and toss to mix. Serve at once.

Note Gai choy or mustard cabbage is also done the same way. It has thick, bright green stems and a tangy, mustard-like flavour.

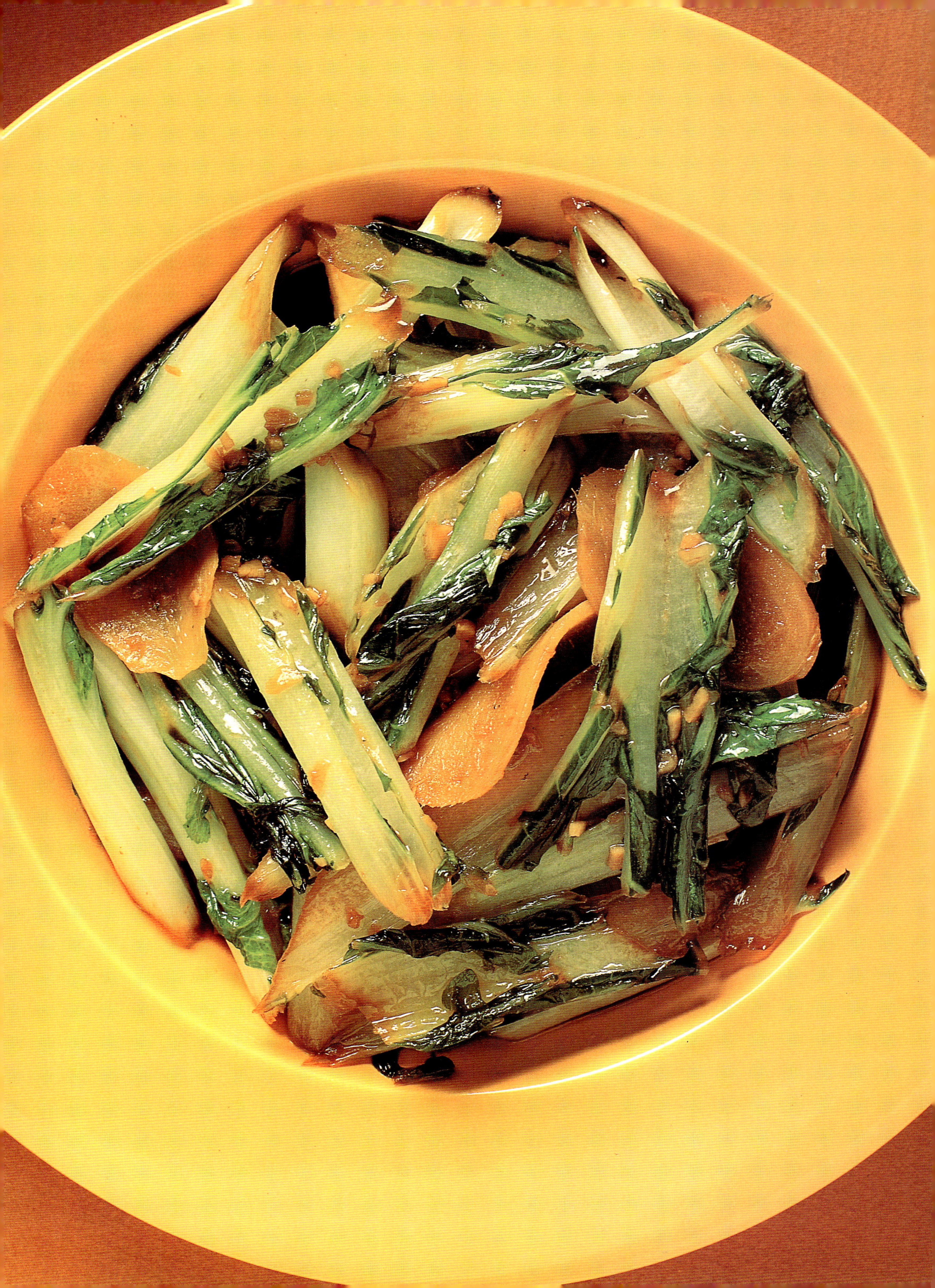

cabbage in coconut milk

serves 6

half a tightly packed cabbage
2 tablespoons peanut oil
1 onion, finely chopped
2 teaspoons finely chopped garlic
2 sprigs fresh curry leaves or 20 dried curry leaves
420 ml (14 fl oz) coconut milk
2 stems lemon grass or 4 strips lemon rind
2 or 3 whole green chillies
salt to taste
lemon juice, optional

Wash and shred cabbage. Heat oil in a large saucepan or wok and gently fry onion, garlic and curry leaves, stirring frequently until onions are translucent and golden, about 15 minutes. Add coconut milk diluted with 240 ml (8 fl oz) water, lemon grass or rind and whole chillies. Stir as it comes to simmering point. Add cabbage and leave to simmer 10 minutes or until cabbage is tender but still slightly crisp. Check seasoning and add a generous squeeze of lemon juice if preferred. Serve with rice.

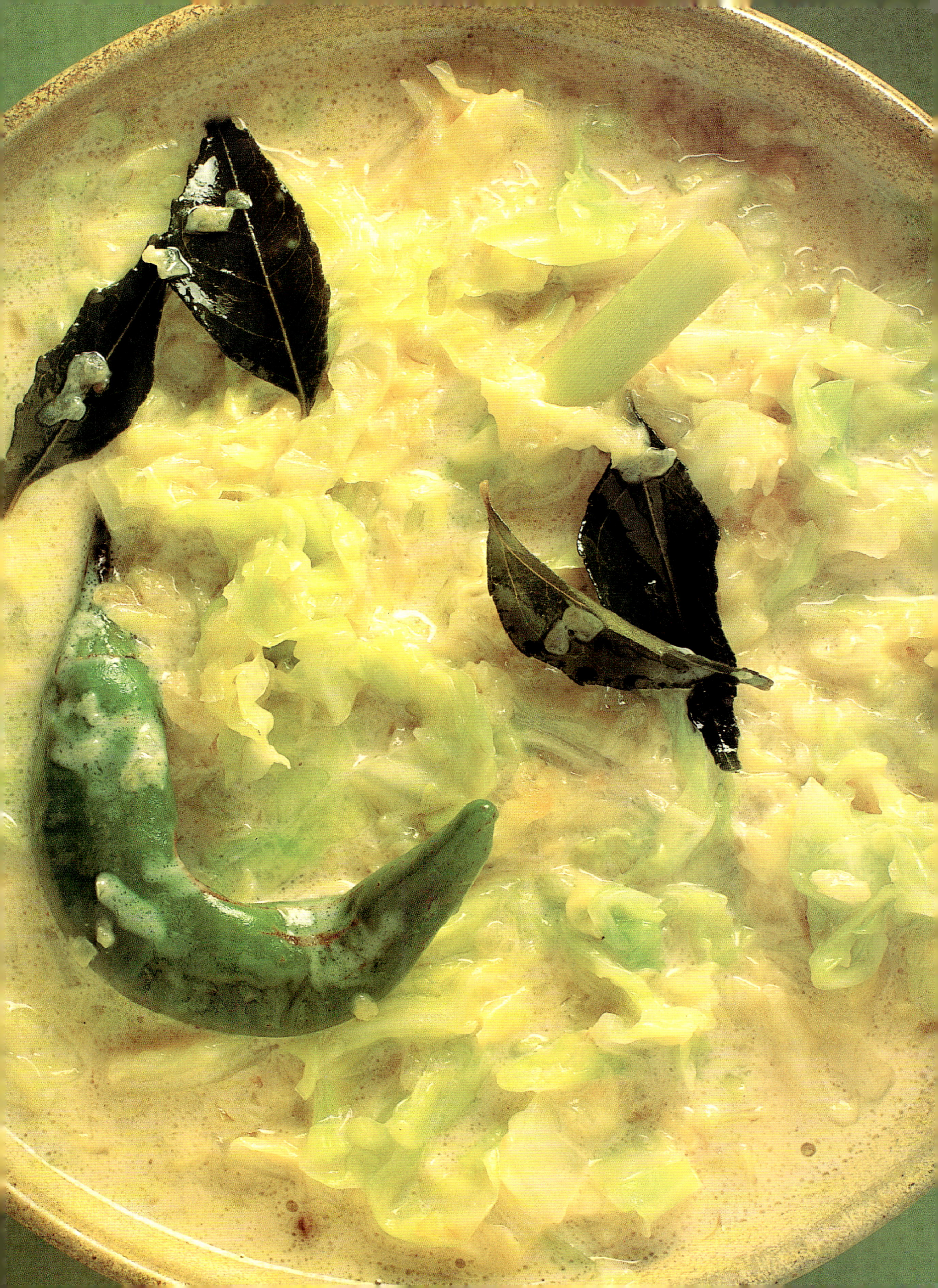

steamed cauliflower

serves 4 to 6

1 medium cauliflower
60 g (2 oz) butter or ghee
2 tablespoons flaked or chopped almonds
1 teaspoon cumin seeds
1 teaspoon black mustard seeds
½ teaspoon kalonji (nigella) seeds
½ teaspoon chilli powder, optional
salt and pepper to taste

Wash cauliflower, trim off stem and make 4 crossways slits in base with sharp knife to allow steam to penetrate. Put 360 ml (12 fl oz) water in a wok and place the cauliflower in it. Bring quickly to the boil, cover and steam for 10 minutes or until just tender enough to be pierced with a skewer. Lift onto serving dish.

Wash and dry wok and melt butter or ghee. Fry almonds and whole seeds until almonds are golden and seeds fragrant. Add chilli powder, salt and pepper just before removing from heat, pour over cauliflower and serve with chapatis, parathas or rice.

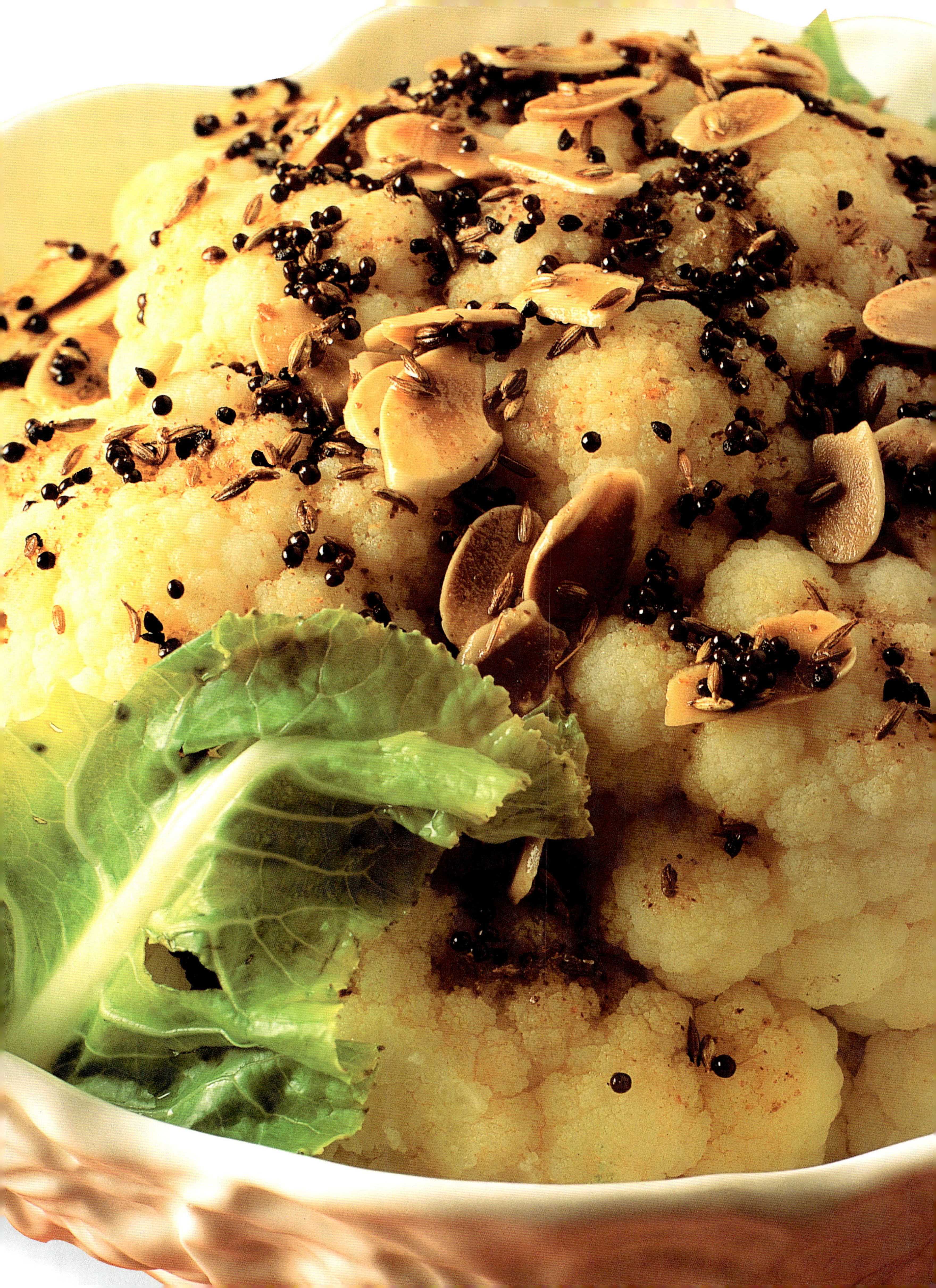

leeks with chilli

serves 4 to 6

2 large leeks
2 tablespoons oil
2 fresh chillies, seeded and sliced
½ teaspoon turmeric
½ teaspoon chilli powder
½ teaspoon salt or to taste

Wash leeks thoroughly, slitting them lengthways and making sure there is no sand or grit lurking between the leaves. Cut off any old or yellow leaves, but all green leaves are used in this recipe as well as the white portions. With a sharp knife slice leeks very finely.

Heat oil in a large saucepan. Add leeks, stir over medium heat for 5 minutes, then add remaining ingredients and mix. Cover pan, turn heat low and cook for 25 minutes or until leeks are very tender and reduced in volume, stirring occasionally. Uncover and cook until no liquid remains. Serve as an accompaniment to rice and curry.

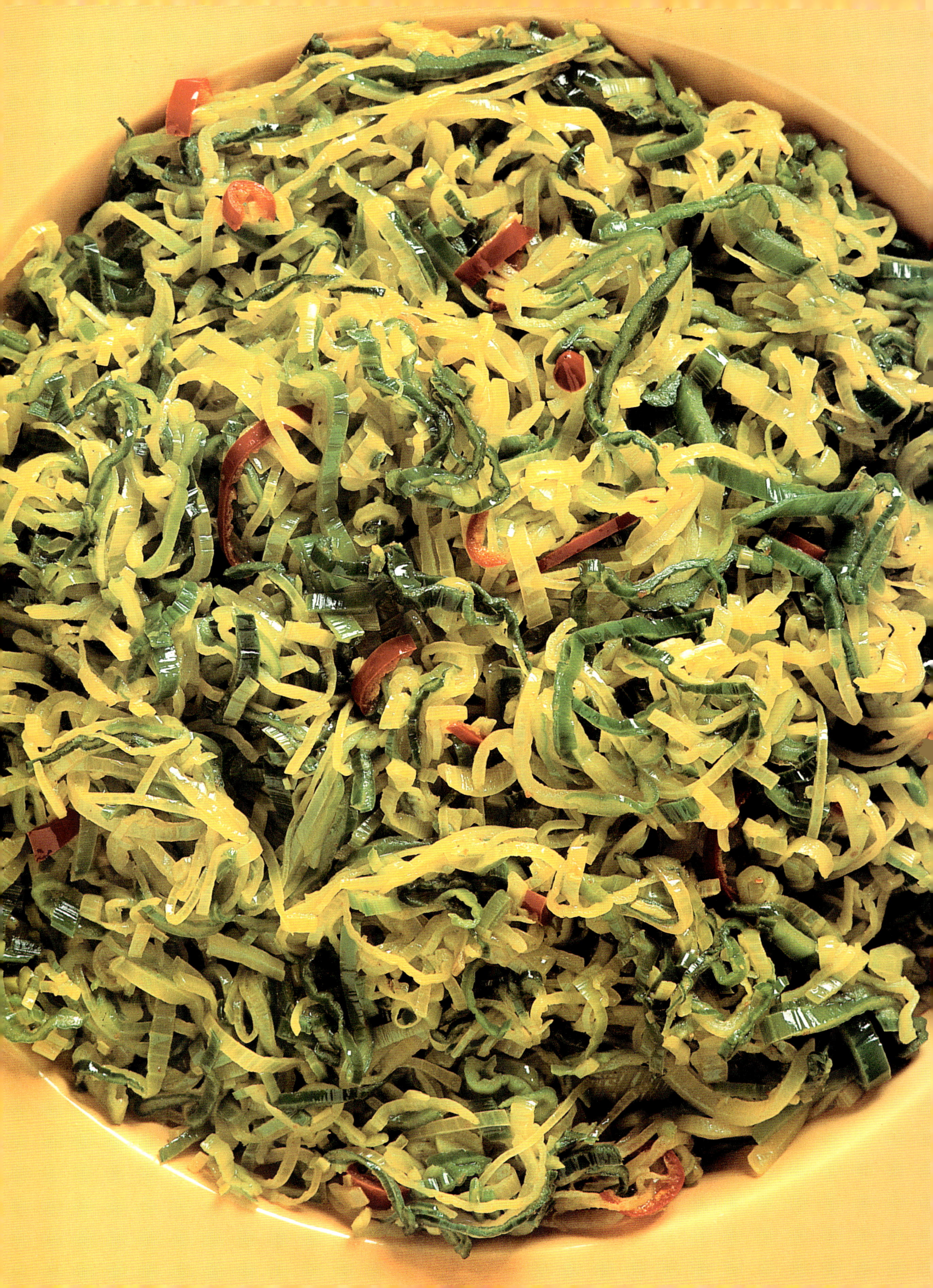

water convolvulus in sweet gravy

In Chinese territory you'd ask for Ong Choy, in Thailand this is Pak Boong, but almost everywhere it answers to the common name of kangkung (u as in 'put'). If it is unavailable substitute chicory or watercress.

serves 4 to 6

- 500 g (1 lb) water convolvulus or kangkung
- 420 ml (14 fl oz) canned coconut milk
- 1 finely sliced onion
- 2 teaspoons finely chopped garlic
- 3 slices fresh ginger
- 2 slices fresh or brined galangal
- ½ teaspoon ground turmeric
- ½ teaspoon salt or to taste
- 2 or 3 fresh green chillies
- 1 tablespoon palm sugar or brown sugar

Wash greens well and discard any tough stems. In a saucepan put coconut milk and an equal amount of water with remaining ingredients. Bring to boil, stirring, then simmer for a further 15 minutes, uncovered. Add greens and simmer for a further 15 minutes. For more substance, add 2 small potatoes, peeled and diced at the beginning of the cooking time. Serve with rice.

cooked green salad

Salad is not just lettuce, nor does it have to be raw. Try using finely shredded parsley, tender passionfruit leaves, radish leaves or piquantly sour sorrel leaves. If you are aware of which wild leaves are good to eat, these will provide more choices.

serves 4

- 60 g (2 oz) edible green leaves
- 1 small onion, finely chopped
- 1 or 2 sliced chillies, optional
- ½ teaspoon turmeric
- 6 tablespoons finely grated fresh coconut (or desiccated coconut)
- lime or lemon juice to taste
- salt to taste

Wash and finely shred leaves and combine with all ingredients except coconut in a saucepan with well-fitting lid. Add 2 tablespoons water, cover tightly and steam over low heat for 5 to 8 minutes. Uncover, stir in coconut and toss over low heat until coconut has absorbed liquid. Serve with rice.

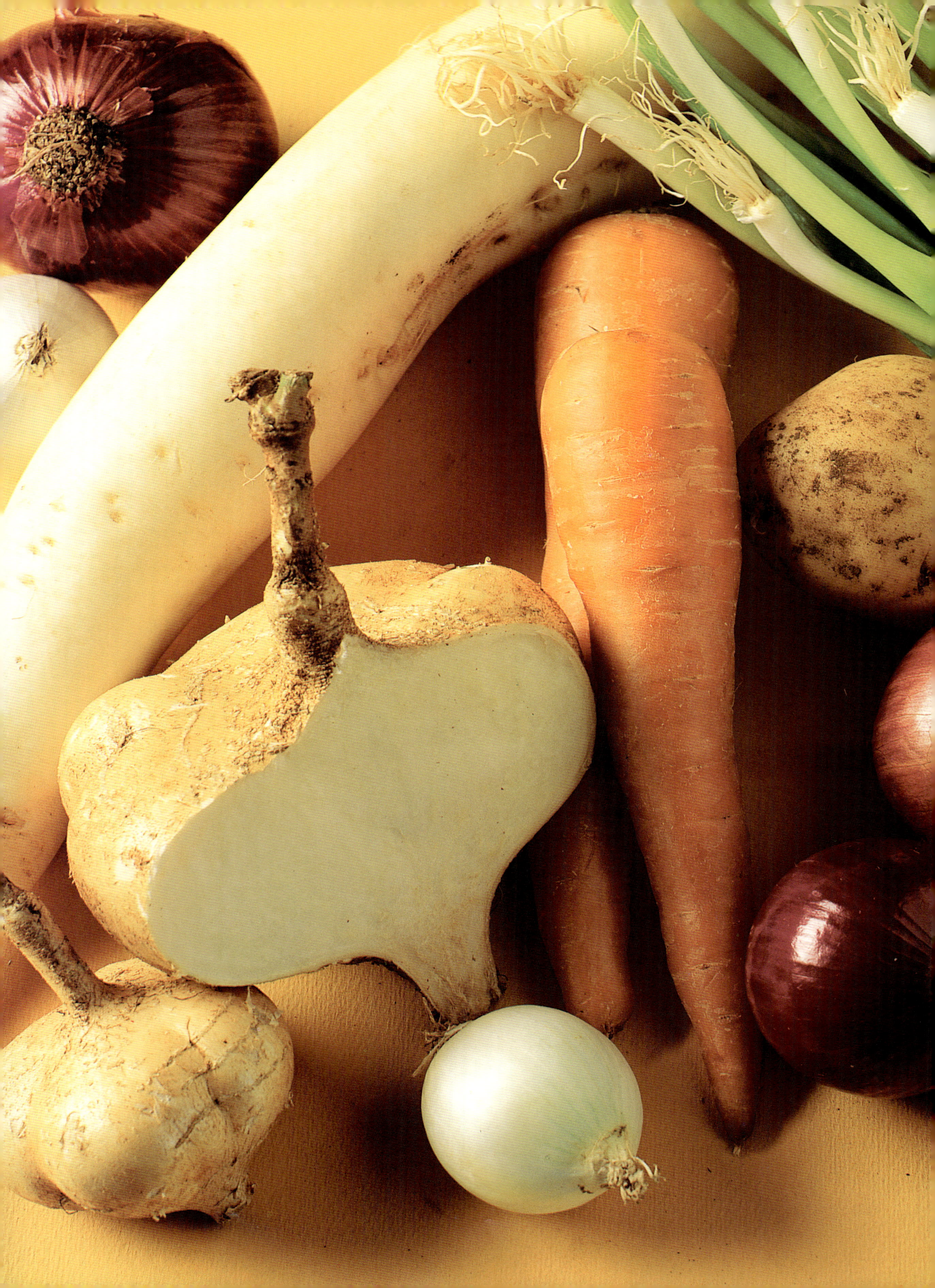

Potatoes, carrots, beetroot, turnips, yams, onions and garlic all belong to this group of underground vegetables, which are the staple of many cultures. Try to imagine what the food of any country would be without the wonderful flavours imparted by onions and garlic. Onions can be used raw in salads, crisp and fresh and full of bite, or they may have their fierceness diminished by soaking in salt and rinsing them. Or they can be cooked gently for a long time, bringing out other nuances of flavour and caramelising their sugar content to give a totally different result. Garlic may be used raw and crushed, in tiny amounts, to add a special zip to a salad or relish. Or it may be cooked for a long while until soft and sweet, with a personality totally different from its raw brashness – in fact, it is a vegetable when treated thus. And is there a cuisine that does not use that great staple, the potato? I firmly believe there are more ways to cook potatoes in India than there are in Ireland!

steamed potatoes

serves 4 to 6

750 g (1½ lb) small new potatoes
1 onion, roughly chopped
2 cloves garlic, chopped
1½ teaspoons chopped fresh ginger
1 teaspoon salt, or to taste
1½ tablespoons ghee or oil
1 cinnamon stick
4 cardamom pods, bruised
2 whole cloves
1 teaspoon ground turmeric

garnish
1 teaspoon toasted and crushed cumin seeds
180 ml (6 fl oz) yoghurt
1 teaspoon Garam Masala (see p. 4)
3 tablespoons chopped fresh coriander

Wash but do not peel potatoes. Boil for 5 minutes, drain and prick all over with a fine skewer.

In a blender or food processor, purée onion, garlic, ginger with salt and 3 tablespoons water. Heat ghee in a heavy saucepan and add cinnamon, cardamom and cloves. Fry for 2 minutes, stirring, then add turmeric and fry for a further minute. Add puréed mixture and cook, stirring, for about 3 minutes or until fragrant.

Add potatoes, cover pan and steam over very low heat for 15 minutes or until potatoes are cooked. Remove whole spices.

To make garnish, combine cumin, yoghurt and Garam Masala. Spoon over potatoes and sprinkle with fresh coriander. Serve with chapatis or rice. This dish is also good with grilled fish.

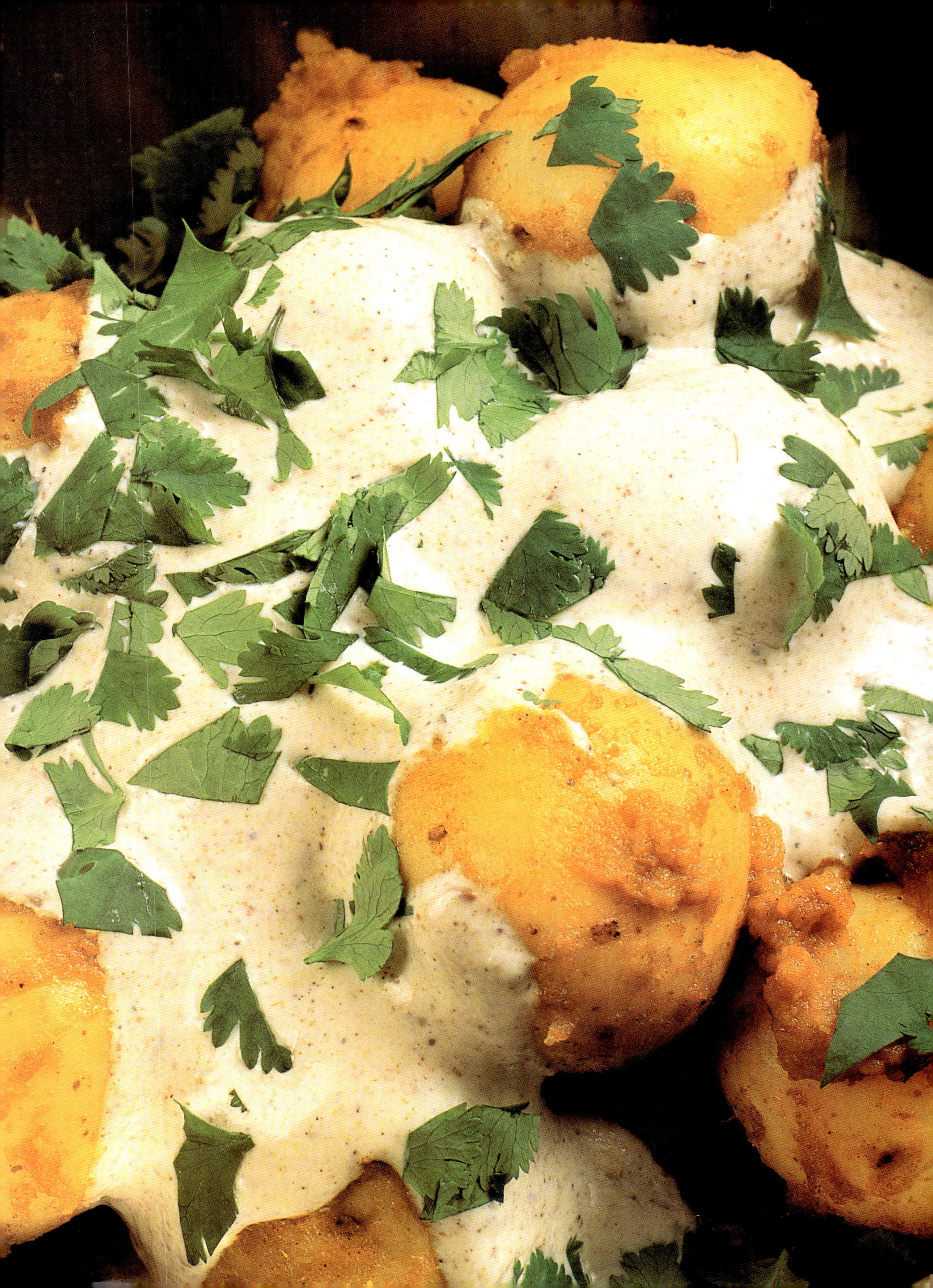

sweet-sour potatoes

serves 4 to 6

- 750 g (1½ lb) potatoes
- 2 tablespoons ghee or oil
- 1 teaspoon black mustard seeds
- 2 fresh chillies, sliced
- 2 teaspoons ground coriander
- 1 teaspoon ground cumin
- ¼ teaspoon ground turmeric
- ½ teaspoon chilli powder or to taste
- ½ teaspoon salt or to taste
- 1 tablespoon dried tamarind pulp
- 2 teaspoons palm sugar or brown sugar

Peel and dice potatoes. In a heavy saucepan heat ghee or oil and fry mustard seeds until they pop. Add chillies and ground spices and stir for 30 seconds or until fragrant. Add potatoes, sprinkle with salt and about 3 tablespoons water, cover pan tightly and cook on very low heat for 15 minutes. Meanwhile, soak tamarind pulp in 60 ml (2 fl oz) hot water and squeeze to dissolve pulp. Strain out seeds and fibres. Dissolve sugar in tamarind liquid. Add to potatoes, stir gently, cover and cook for a further 10 minutes or until potatoes are tender. Serve with chapatis or rice.

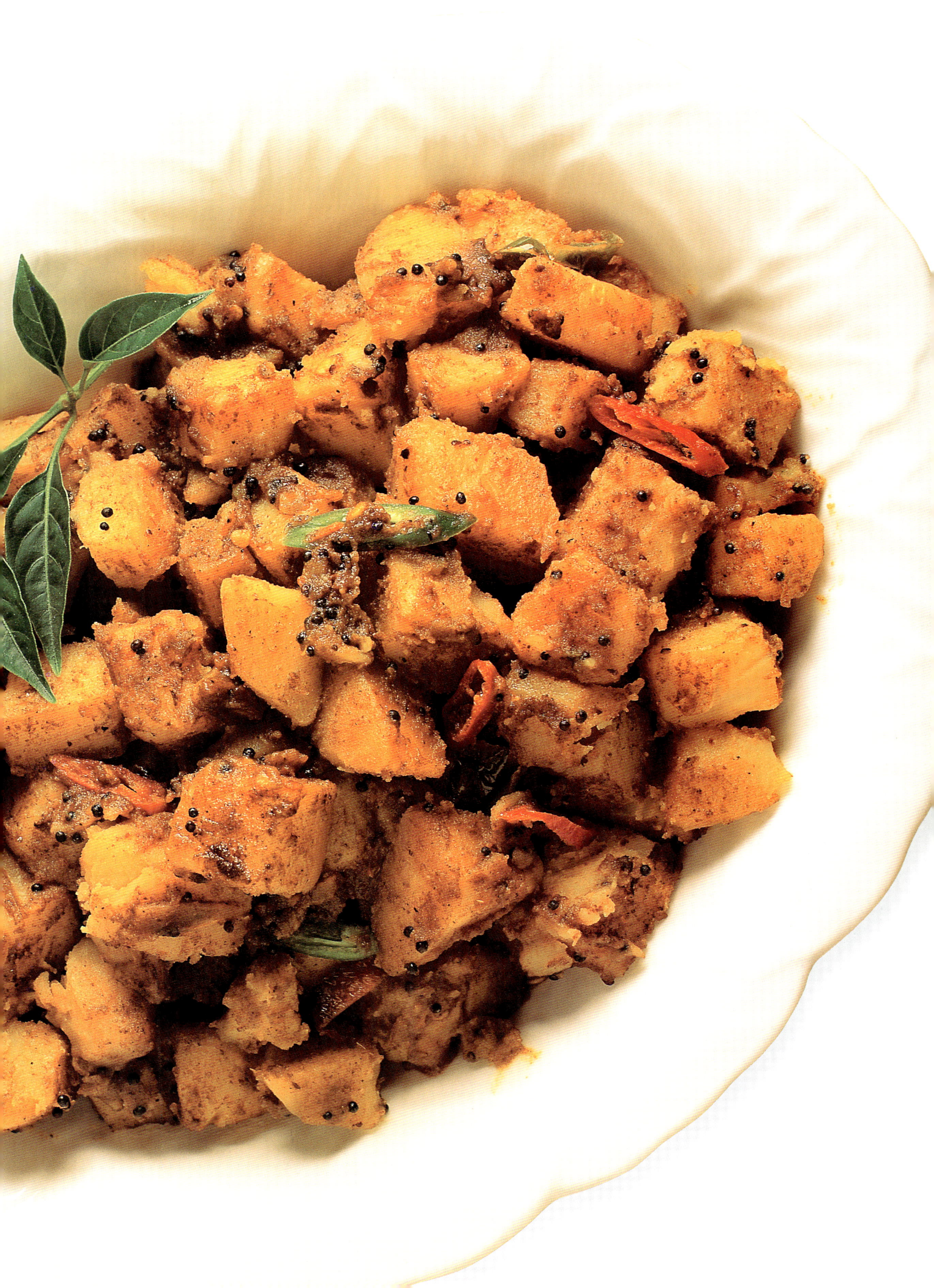

yam curry

Use yams and sweet potatoes in the same way you would use potatoes, judging the cooking time according to variety being used.

serves 4

- 500 g (1 lb) yam or sweet potato
- oil for deep frying
- 1 tablespoon ghee
- 2 medium onions, chopped finely
- 2 teaspoons finely chopped fresh ginger
- 2 fresh red or green chillies, seeded and chopped
- 1 teaspoon ground coriander
- 1 teaspoon ground cumin
- ½ teaspoon Garam Masala (see p. 4)
- 1 teaspoon salt or to taste
- 3 tablespoons chopped fresh coriander
- lemon juice to taste

Peel and slice or dice yam. Soak in lightly salted water for 30 minutes. Drain well and dry thoroughly on paper towels. Heat oil and add ghee to give it flavour. Deep fry yam, not too much at one time, until golden brown. Lift on slotted spoon and drain on paper towels.

Pour off oil, leaving about 2 tablespoons. Fry onion, ginger and chillies over medium heat, stirring occasionally, until onion is soft and golden. Add ground spices and fry for another minute, stirring. Add yams, sprinkle with salt and fresh coriander and toss over low heat for 5 minutes. Add lemon juice to taste. Serve with rice or chapatis.

potato and pea pastries

If you do not want to make your own pastry, you could use 25-cm (10-in) square sheets of spring roll pastry.

makes about 36

pastry
420 g (14 oz) plain flour
1 teaspoon salt
1 tablespoon soft butter or ghee

filling
500 g (1 lb) potatoes, peeled and diced small
1 teaspoon turmeric
150 g (5 oz) fresh or frozen peas
1 small onion, finely chopped
salt to taste
1 teaspoon ground cumin
½ teaspoon Garam Masala (see p. 4)
2 tablespoons lime or lemon juice
oil for deep frying

Prepare pastry by sifting the flour with salt, rub in butter and add 240 ml (8 fl oz) lukewarm water. Mix well to form a soft dough. Knead for 10 minutes, the dough should be smooth and elastic. Wrap in plastic and leave to rest while preparing filling.

Add turmeric to lightly salted water and boil potatoes until tender. Drain. If using fresh peas, cook until tender. If frozen, thaw only. Mix together potatoes, peas and onion with salt, cumin, Garam Masala and lime or lemon juice. Shape the dough into small balls and roll out on a lightly floured surface into 20-cm (8-in) rounds. Cut each round in thirds. Place a tablespoon of filling on one side of each segment, brush around the edges with water. Fold over the pastry to enclose the mixture and press the edges together firmly to form a triangle. Deep fry the pastries a few at a time in hot oil and drain on paper towels. These may be eaten warm or cold, they are nice served with a Tamarind Chutney (see p. 86) for dipping.

Note If using spring roll pastry, cut each 25 cm (10 in) square into 3 equal strips. Place filling at one end of strip and fold diagonally to make triangle. Continue folding until entire strip has been used. Moisten last flap with water and press to stick.

piquant carrots

serves 4

500 g (1 lb) carrots
3 tablespoons oil
2 teaspoons crushed garlic
1 teaspoon turmeric
1 teaspoon ground cumin

2 teaspoons paprika
¼ teaspoon chilli powder, optional
salt to taste
2 teaspoons sugar
2 tablespoons lemon juice

Peel carrots and cut into fine diagonal slices. A food processor does this in no time. Heat oil in a pan with a well-fitting lid and cook garlic slowly until mellow. Add ground spices and stir for 1 minute, then add carrots and mix well. Add 60 ml (2 fl oz) water, cover and steam for 10 minutes or until carrots are tender. Add salt, sugar and lemon juice, mix well and serve at room temperature.

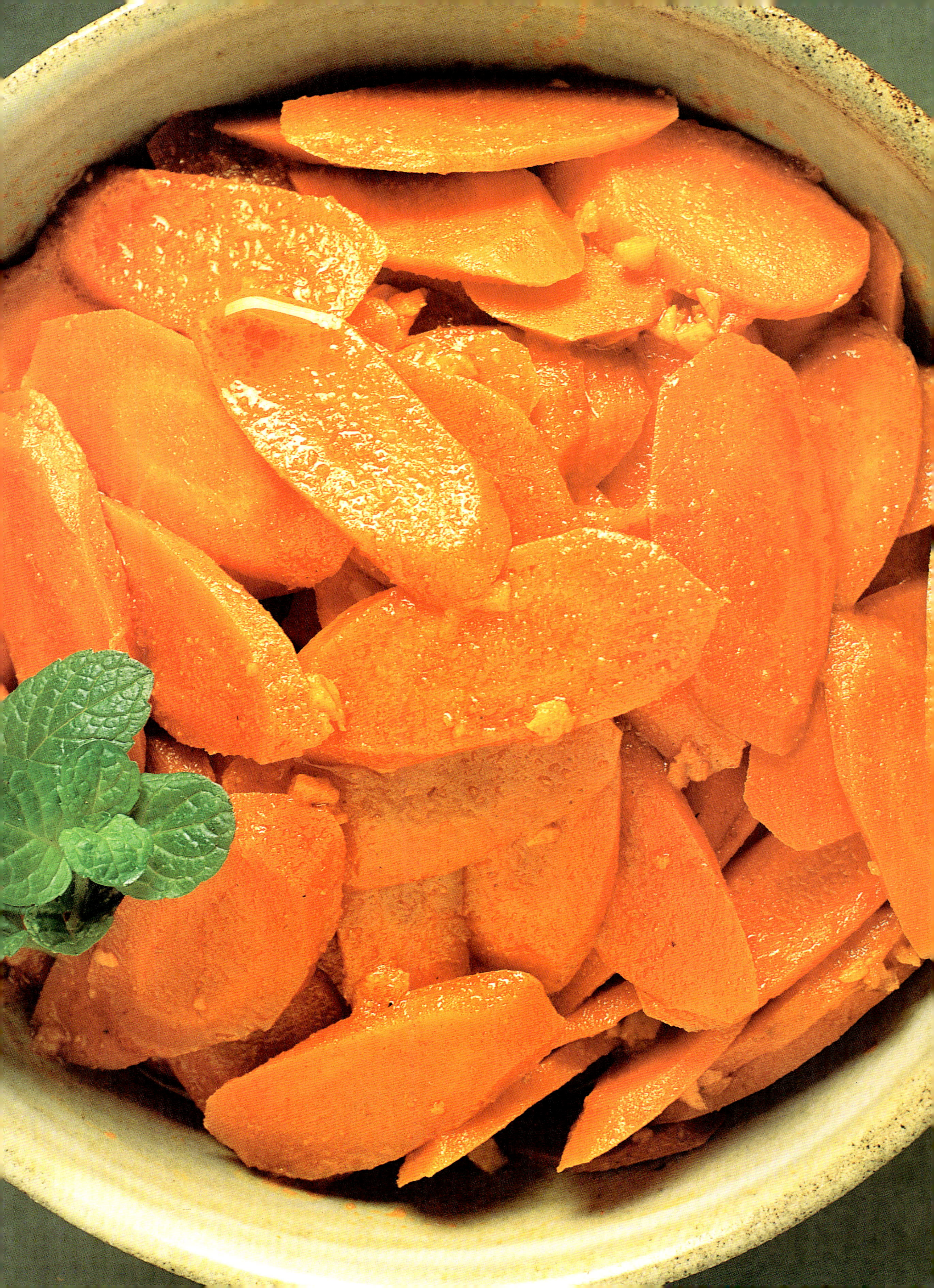

carrot and radish salad

serves 6

- 2 carrots, shredded or cut into short julienne strips
- 1 white radish (daikon), shredded or cut into short julienne strips
- 3 spring onions, including some green tops, sliced
- salt to taste
- 1 tablespoon caster sugar
- 80 ml (2½ fl oz) rice vinegar or white wine vinegar
- 1 teaspoon wasabi (green horseradish) powder

Put carrots, radish and spring onions in a bowl. Sprinkle salt over and rub into ingredients. Cover with cold water and let stand for 20 to 30 minutes. Drain and rinse again with cold water. Drain, squeezing out as much water as possible. Add sugar and rub in well. Sprinkle with vinegar and wasabi mixed with 1 tablespoon water. Mix well. (If wasabi is unavailable substitute hot English mustard.) Transfer to a bowl and serve.

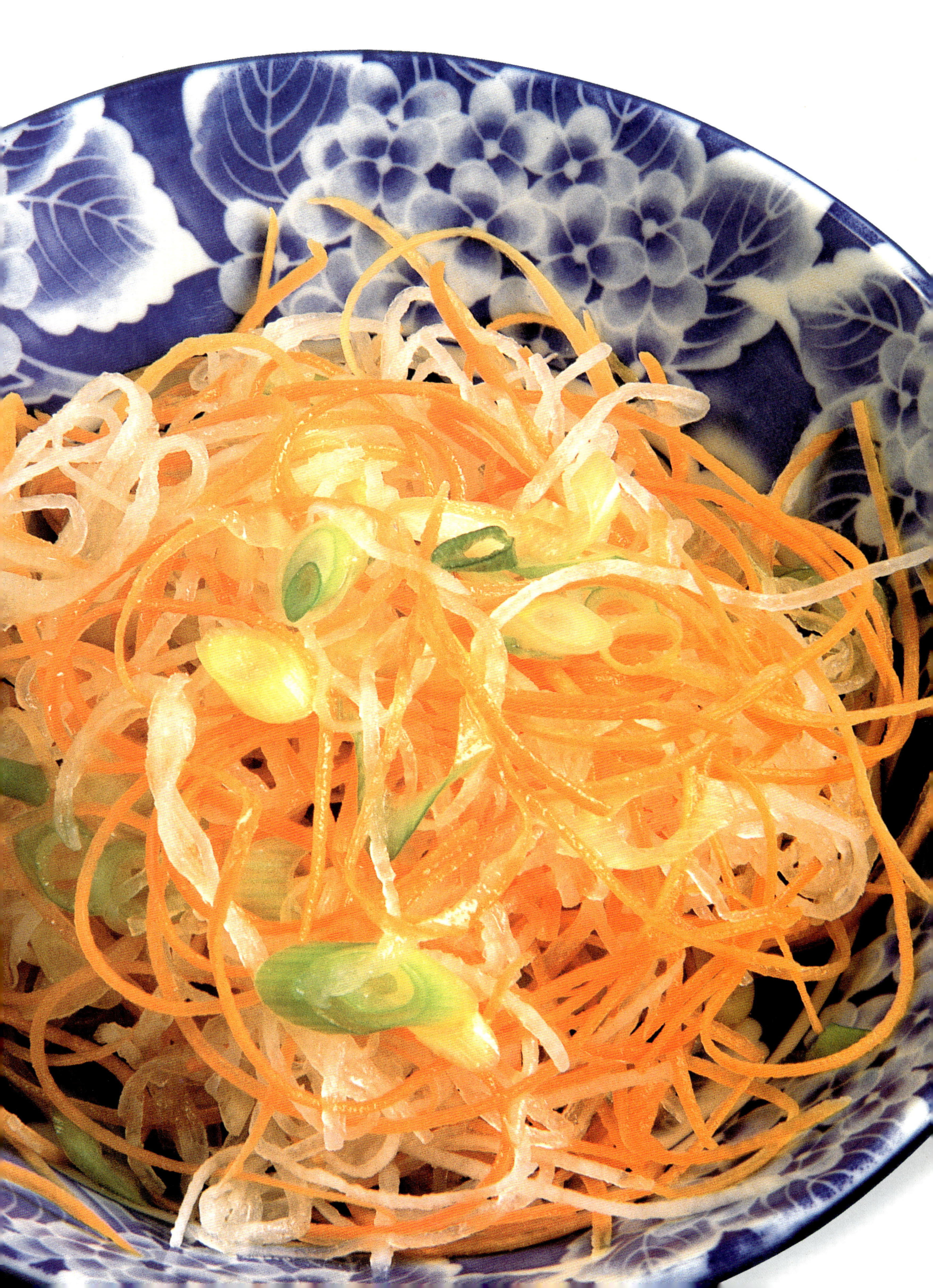

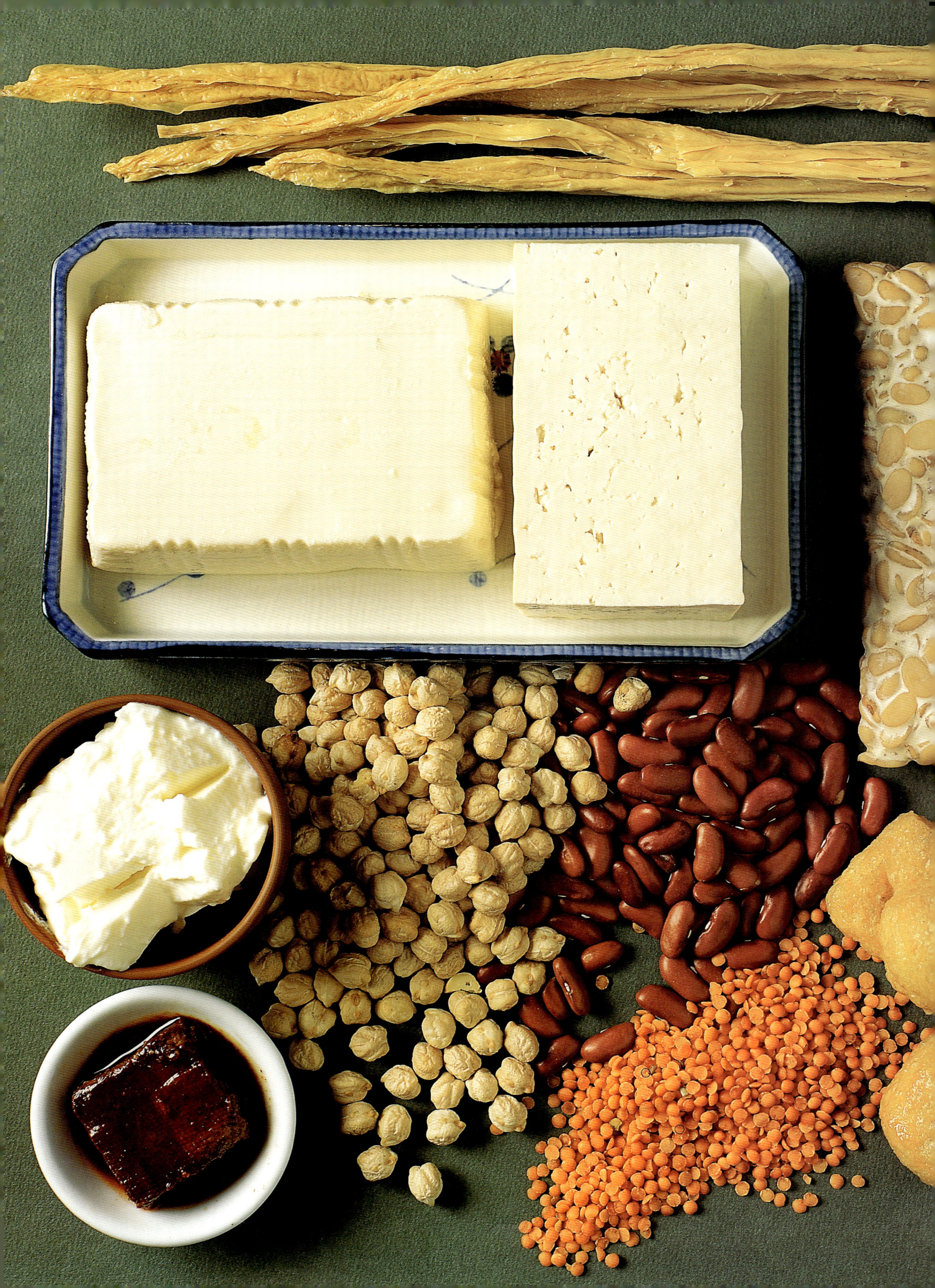

Protein sources in vegetarian meals come from cheese, milk, eggs, yoghurt, lentils and soy bean products.

Fresh bean curd comes in various forms – soft, firm, fried. Look in the refrigerator section of Asian shops or health food stores. Fermented soy bean cakes (tempeh) are sold frozen. Dried bean curd (in sheets or sticks) is in packets and has a long shelf life. Red (pickled) bean curd comes in jars and is the Asian equivalent of gorgonzola. It keeps well and a small amount adds a lot of zip to a dish.

Fresh cheese for Indian dishes is quick and easy to make. Even quicker is to buy baked ricotta. It is suited to recipes where cheese is cut in cubes, but not a recipe in which the cheese has to be moulded.

Lentils and dried peas or beans make delicious soups, purées, curries, rissoles, salads or braised dishes.

In this section, you will also find delectable dishes that combine different types of vegetables.

pakorhas

These crisp, lightly battered and fried vegetable fritters are popular with everyone – even those who dislike vegetables will be asking for more!

serves 4 as appetiser

- 60 g (2 oz) besan (chick pea flour)
- 90 g (3 oz) self-raising flour
- 2 tablespoons ground rice
- 1 teaspoon Garam Masala (see p. 4)
- ½ teaspoon ajowan seeds
- ½ teaspoon ground turmeric
- ¼ teaspoon chilli powder, optional
- ½ teaspoon salt
- fine slices of potato, onion, cauliflower, eggplant, washed and dried leaves of English spinach, sorrel
- peanut oil for deep-frying

Combine flours, spices and salt with 240 ml (8 fl oz) water and beat to a smooth batter of coating consistency.

Prepare vegetables. Small potatoes are better than large. Peel and slice them very thinly. Peel onion, keeping the root end on and cutting in thin slices lengthways so there is a bit of root left to hold layers together. Cauliflower should be sliced thinly with a piece of stem to hold florets together. Eggplant (again small, rather than large) is left unpeeled and sliced fairly thickly. If large, slices may be halved. Wash leaves and dry thoroughly on paper towels – if large, cut in 2 or 3 pieces. (If you have a grape vine, try some very small, tender vine leaves – they are delicious!)

Heat oil for deep frying and dip a few pieces of vegetable at a time in batter, then drop in oil and fry until golden brown and crisp. Lift out with a slotted spoon and drain on paper towels. Serve with Tamarind Chutney (see p. 86) or Fresh Mint Chutney.

Note Pakorhas are also made with finely diced vegetables, mixed into batter and fried in spoonfuls.

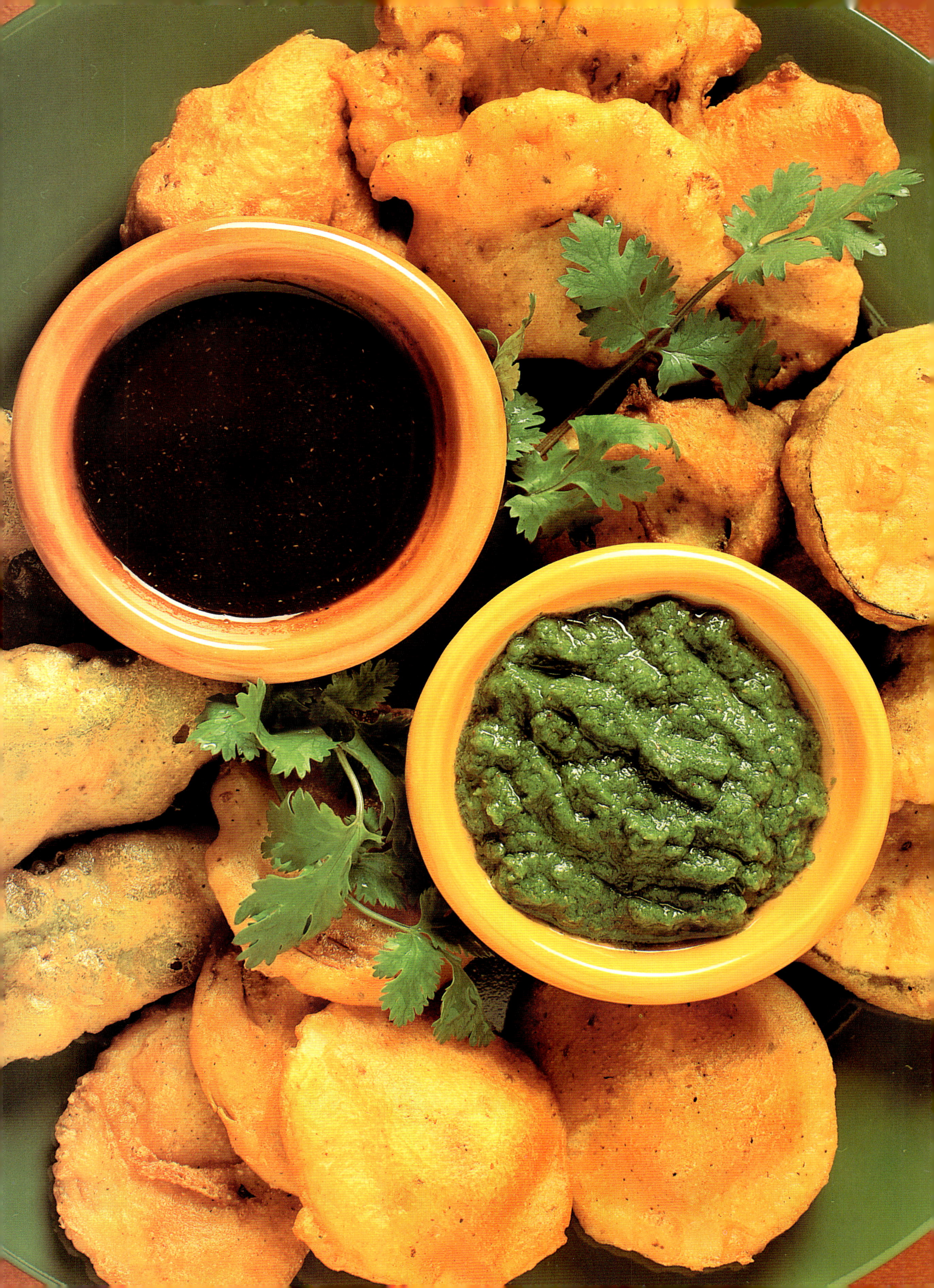

braised vegetable combination

A famous Chinese vegetarian dish. I have eaten it several times, including a deluxe version in a Buddhist monastery high on a mountain on one of the outlying islands of Hong Kong, in a superb, totally vegetarian meal, with rare ingredients. This version is pleasing and entirely attainable.

serves 4 to 6

- 120 g (4 oz) dried bean curd sticks
- 16–18 dried shiitake (Chinese) mushrooms
- 30 dried lily buds (golden needles)
- 15 g (½ oz) dried wood fungus
- 2 canned winter bamboo shoots
- 1 canned lotus root
- 1 small can water chestnuts
- 500 g (1 lb) fresh asparagus
- 1 can baby corn
- 3 tablespoons peanut oil
- 3 tablespoons light soy sauce
- 2 tablespoons hoi sin sauce
- 1 whole star anise
- 2 teaspoons cornflour
- 2 teaspoons oriental sesame oil
- 2 teaspoons sugar

There's a lot of soaking of dried ingredients, so line up some bowls. Snap bean curd sticks into bite-sized pieces and soak in cold water for 20 minutes. Drain, return to bowl and pour boiling water over. Leave to cool. Soak dried mushrooms in very hot water to cover for at least 30 minutes. (If they are thick, high quality shiitake, it will take about an hour for them to soak through, but they are worth the wait.) Drain, squeeze out excess moisture (save soaking liquid) and trim off stems.

Soak lily buds in warm water for 30 minutes, drain, pinch off stem ends if tough and tie a knot in each or cut in halves. Soak wood fungus in cold water for 20 minutes, drain and cut into bite-sized pieces, trimming off any gritty bits.

Slice bamboo shoots, lotus root and water chestnuts. Trim ends off asparagus, peel lower stem and cut in short lengths. Blanch asparagus for 2 minutes in boiling water, then drop into iced water to set the colour. Drain baby corn.

Heat wok, add peanut oil and when very hot, fry well-drained bean curd, mushrooms and lily buds for 3 to 4 minutes. Add soy and hoi sin sauces and 480 ml (16 fl oz) mushroom soaking liquid. Add star anise, bring to the boil, then cover and simmer gently for 20 minutes. Add bamboo shoots, lotus root, water chestnuts and simmer for 10 minutes. Stir cornflour mixed with a tablespoon of cold water into the liquid until it boils and thickens. Lastly add asparagus, baby corn, wood fungus, sugar and sesame oil and mix well. Serve with rice.

Note Lily buds are available fresh in season and make a bright, attractive addition to the dish. These are the buds of a variety of orange and yellow day lilies (*Hemerocallis* spp.). If using them fresh they do not need soaking and the stem ends don't have to be trimmed, being crisply tender. Look for them in Asian shops around autumn.

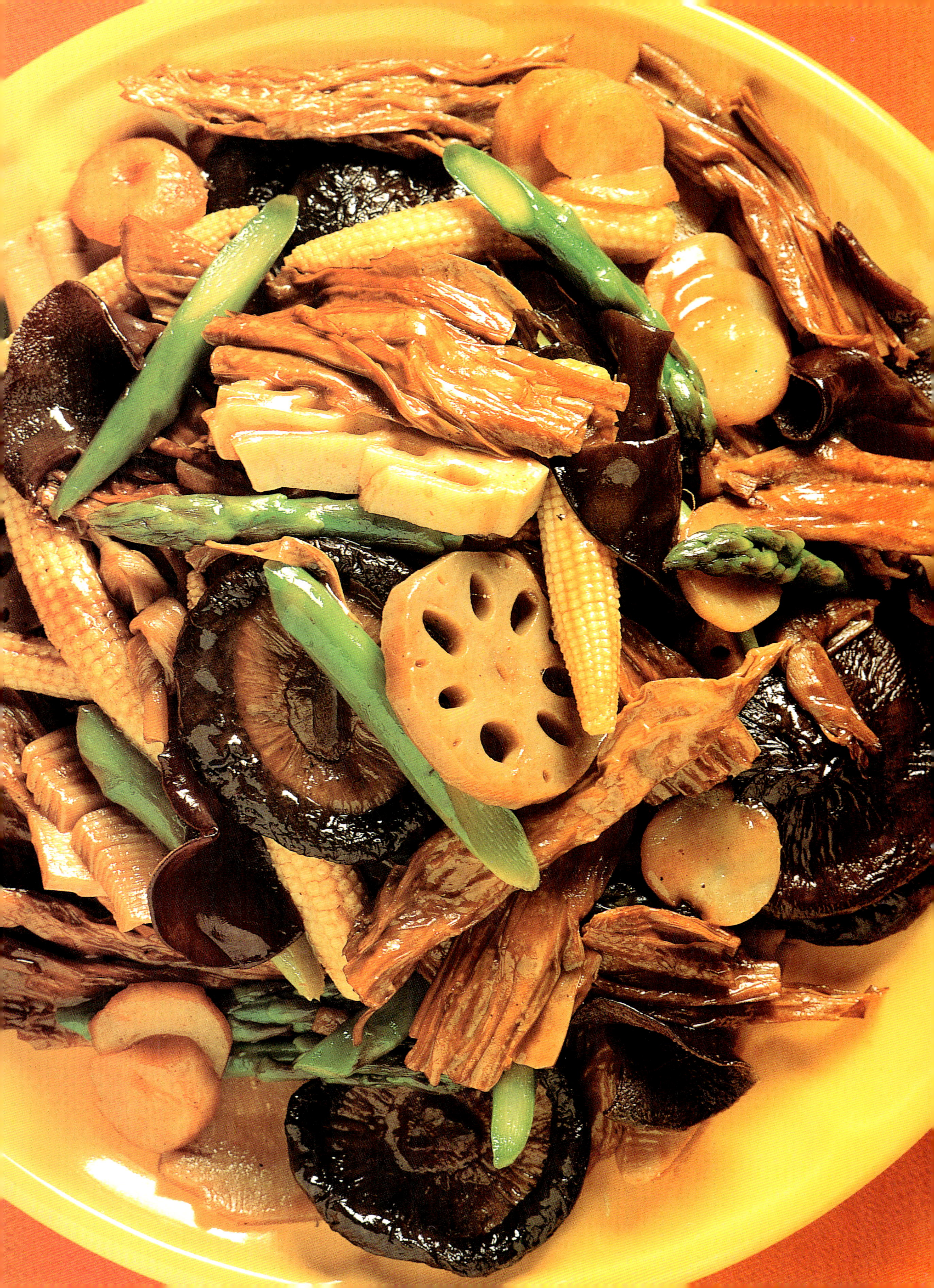

eggplant purée with chick peas

serves 6

- 210 g (7 oz) dried chick peas
- 4 cardamom pods
- 2 large eggplants
- 2 tablespoons oil or ghee
- 2 large onions, finely chopped
- 2 teaspoons finely chopped ginger
- 2 teaspoons ground coriander
- 2 teaspoons ground cumin
- ½ teaspoon turmeric
- 2 large tomatoes, chopped
- 1 teaspoon of salt

Soak chick peas in water for at least 6 hours. Put chick peas in a heavy saucepan, cover by at least 2.5 cm (1 in) of fresh water and add cardamom pods, bruised. Bring to a simmer and cook, covered, for 1 hour or until tender but still holding their shape.

Grill eggplants over a barbecue or under a preheated griller until skins are blackened. Cool, peel and discard skin. Chop flesh roughly.

In a heavy saucepan heat oil and cook onions and ginger over gentle heat, stirring occasionally, for 20 minutes or until onions are soft and translucent, and turn golden. Add ground spices and fry, stirring, for 1 minute, then add eggplant, salt and tomatoes, stir well, cover and cook for 30 minutes. Stir in drained chick peas and simmer, covered, a further 15 to 20 minutes. Taste and add salt if necessary. Serve with rice or chapatis.

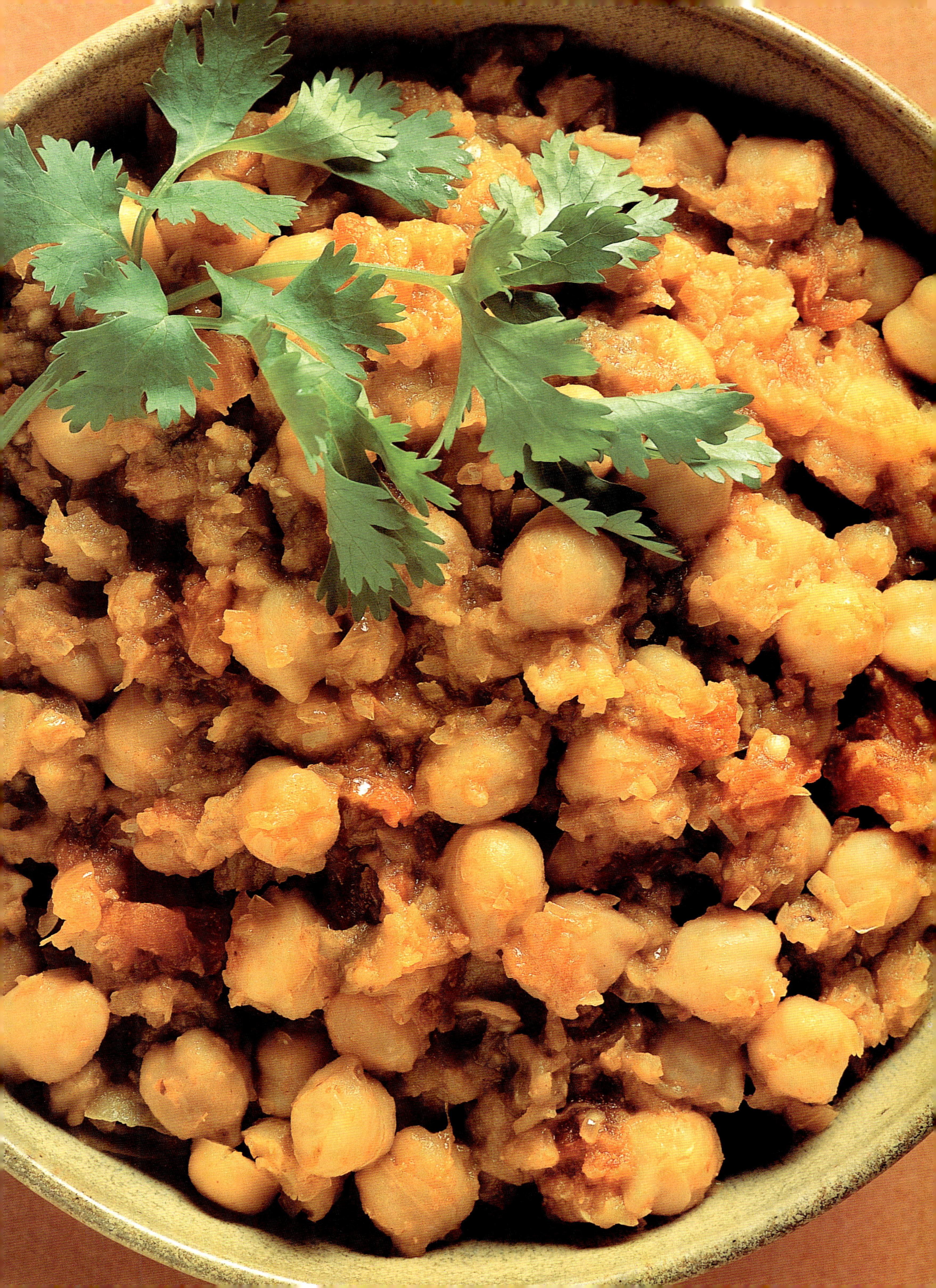

spiced mixed vegetables

Vary the vegetables in this dish but whatever you do, don't overcook.

serves 6

- 2 yellow squash, halved
- 240 g (8 oz) butternut pumpkin, peeled and diced
- 240 g (8 oz) green beans, topped, tailed and cut in half
- quarter of a cauliflower, cut in florets
- half a small cabbage, sliced thickly
- 3 tablespoons peanut oil
- ½ teaspoon cumin seeds
- ½ teaspoon black mustard seeds
- sprig of fresh curry leaves
- 1 onion, finely chopped
- 2 cloves garlic, chopped
- 1 teaspoon finely grated fresh ginger
- 1 teaspoon ground turmeric
- ½ teaspoon Garam Masala (see p. 4)
- salt to taste

Prepare vegetables and have them ready. In large saucepan heat oil and fry cumin, mustard seeds and curry leaves for 1 minute, stirring constantly. Add onion, garlic and ginger and fry until onion is soft. Stir in turmeric and Garam Masala.

Add squash, pumpkin, beans and cauliflower. Cook, stirring, over medium heat until vegetables are half cooked, then add cabbage and toss together until vegetables are tender but still crisp. Sprinkle with salt and mix well. Serve immediately with rice.

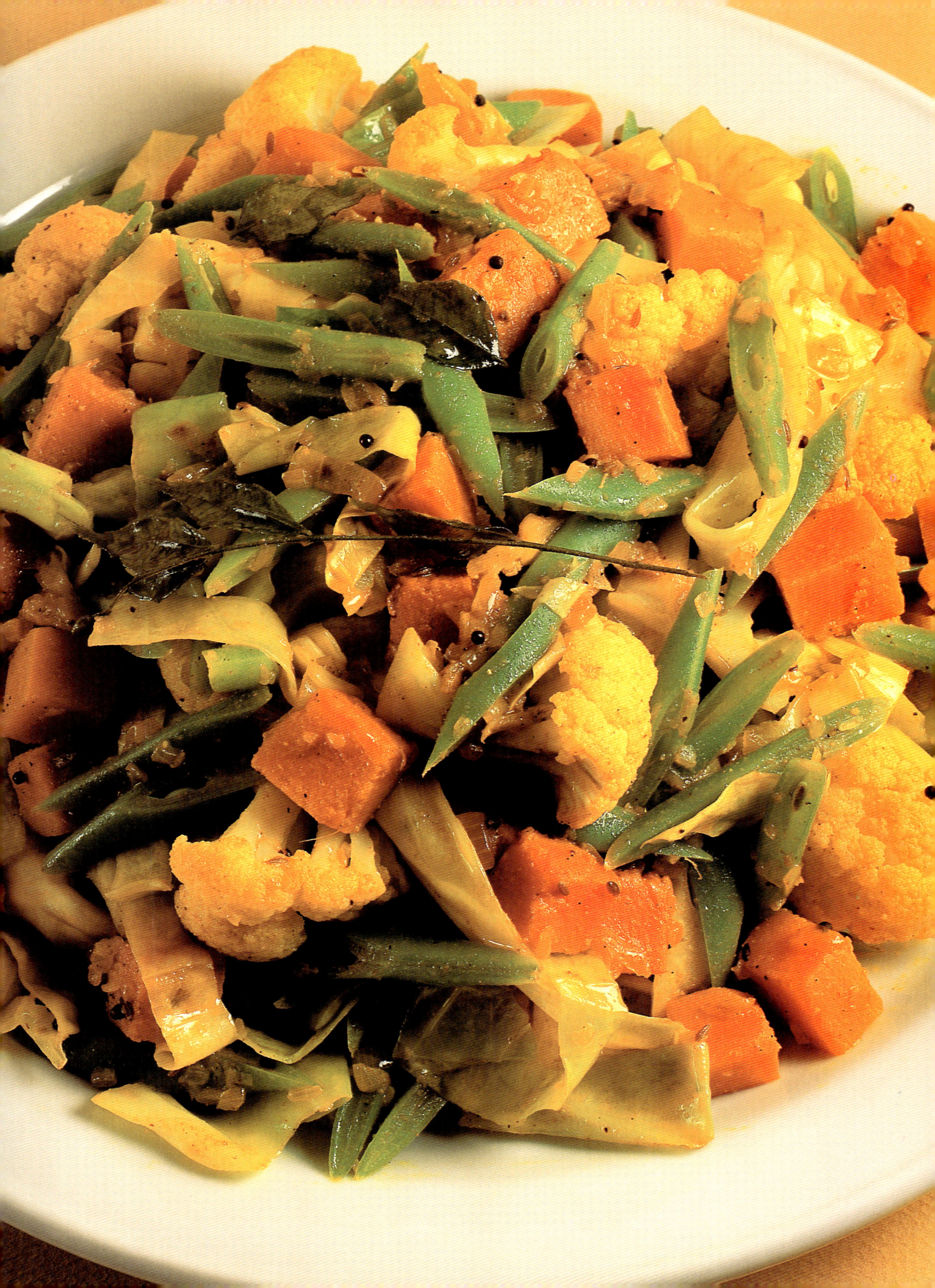

gado gado

A restaurant favourite as a first course, this also makes a satisfying main course and is served at room temperature with plain rice.

serves 6

- 6 medium potatoes, boiled
- 250 g (8 oz) fresh bean sprouts
- 500 g (1 lb) green beans
- 3 carrots
- ½ small cabbage
- 1 green cucumber
- small bunch watercress
- 6 hard-boiled eggs

peanut sauce

- 8 tablespoons crunchy peanut butter
- 1 teaspoon crushed garlic
- 2 teaspoons palm sugar or dark brown sugar
- 2 tablespoons dark soy sauce
- 2 tablespoons lemon juice
- 1 tablespoon shrimp paste
- 2 tablespoons crisp fried onions
- canned coconut milk or water for thinning

Peel potatoes and cut in slices. Wash bean sprouts and pinch off straggly tails. Pour boiling water over sprouts in colander, then rinse under cold water; leave to drain. Trim beans and cut in diagonal slices. Cook in lightly salted boiling water until tender but still crisp. Scrub carrots and cut into thin strips: cook until just tender. Drain. Slice cabbage, discarding tough centre stem. Blanch briefly in boiling salted water, drain and refresh under cold water. Score skin of cucumber with a fork and cut into very thin slices. Wash watercress and break into sprigs, discarding tough stalks. Chill until crisp.

Place watercress on a large platter and arrange the various vegetables in separate sections on top. Surround with slices of cucumber and arrange wedges of hard-boiled egg in centre. Serve cold, accompanied by Peanut Sauce and plain rice. The sauce is spooned over individual servings.

Peanut sauce

Place peanut butter in a saucepan with 240 ml (8 fl oz) water, stirring over gentle heat until well mixed. Remove from heat and stir in remaining ingredients. Add a little coconut milk or water to thin to a thick pouring consistency. Add more salt and lemon juice if needed.

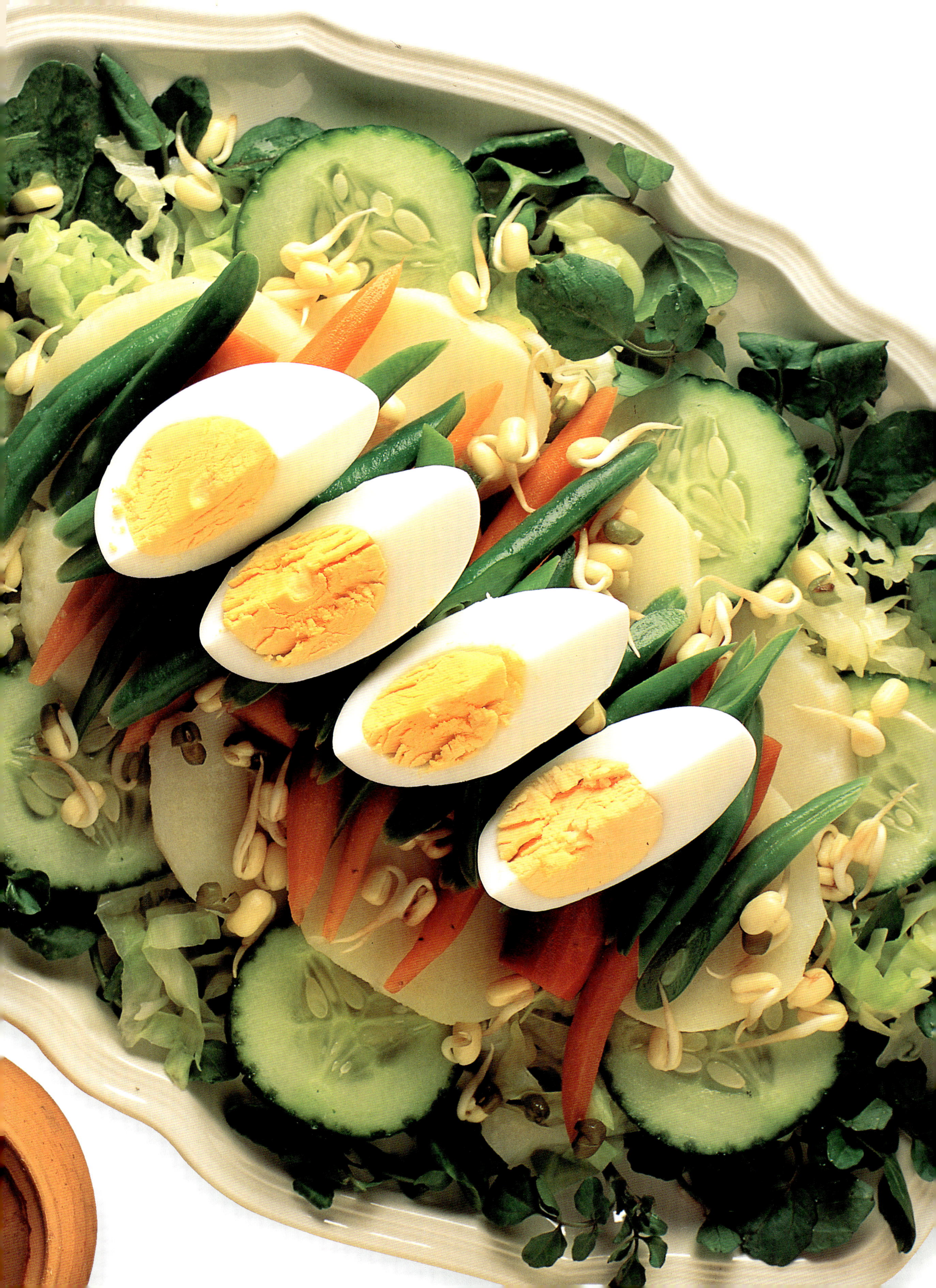

mixed vegetables with coconut

You can use a variety of vegetables for this dish. I suggest carrots, beans, zucchini, pumpkin, capsicum and eggplant, but it is up to you.

serves 6

- 6 cups mixed vegetables, cut into julienne strips
- 3 tablespoons desiccated coconut
- 1 teaspoon cumin seeds
- 1 teaspoon chopped garlic
- 2 fresh green chillies, seeded
- 60 ml (2 fl oz) canned coconut milk
- salt to taste
- 2 sprigs fresh curry leaves or 12 dried curry leaves

In a saucepan boil just enough lightly salted water to cook vegetables. Boil each kind of vegetable separately until tender but still crisp. Remove each batch with a slotted spoon and reserve in a bowl. Re-use water for all vegetables, adding a little more as it boils away – keep quantity small. Reserve cooking liquid. Put desiccated coconut into pan with liquid and when lukewarm, blend with cumin seeds, garlic and chillies on high speed until coconut is very finely ground. Add this mixture to saucepan with coconut milk, 60 ml (2 fl oz) water, salt and curry leaves. Add vegetables, stirring gently to coat and simmer uncovered for 5 minutes. Serve hot with steamed rice.

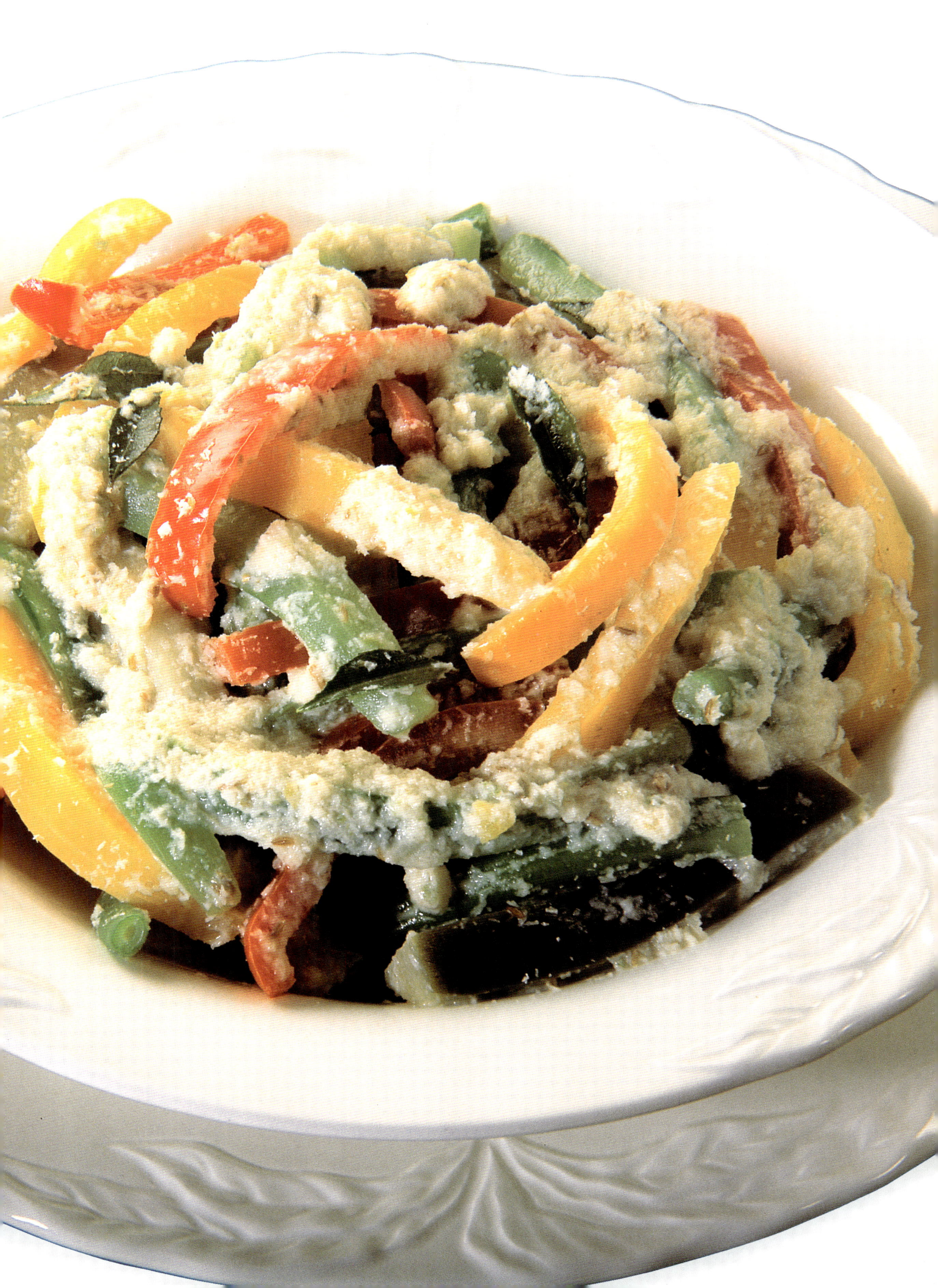

stir-fried eggs with vegetables

serves 4 to 6

4 eggs
salt to taste
240 g (8 oz) Chinese cabbage (wongah bak)
60 g (2 oz) button mushrooms
1 carrot
4 spring onions

2 tablespoons peanut oil
½ teaspoon finely grated fresh ginger
1 small clove garlic, finely chopped
1 tablespoon light soy sauce
½ teaspoon sugar
1 teaspoon oriental sesame oil

Beat eggs and salt together. Halve cabbage leaves lengthways, stack and shred finely. Wipe mushrooms, trim stems and slice. Cut carrot into matchstick strips. Cut spring onions diagonally.

Heat 1 tablespoon peanut oil in a wok. Pour in eggs and stir-fry until set. Transfer to plate. Wipe out wok and heat remaining peanut oil. Add ginger and garlic and stir-fry for a few seconds. Add cabbage, mushrooms and carrot and stir-fry for 1 minute. Cover wok and cook for 1 to 2 minutes until vegetables are half cooked. Add spring onions, soy sauce, sugar and sesame oil. Cover and cook over low heat for 1 minute. Toss through cooked eggs and serve immediately with rice or bread.

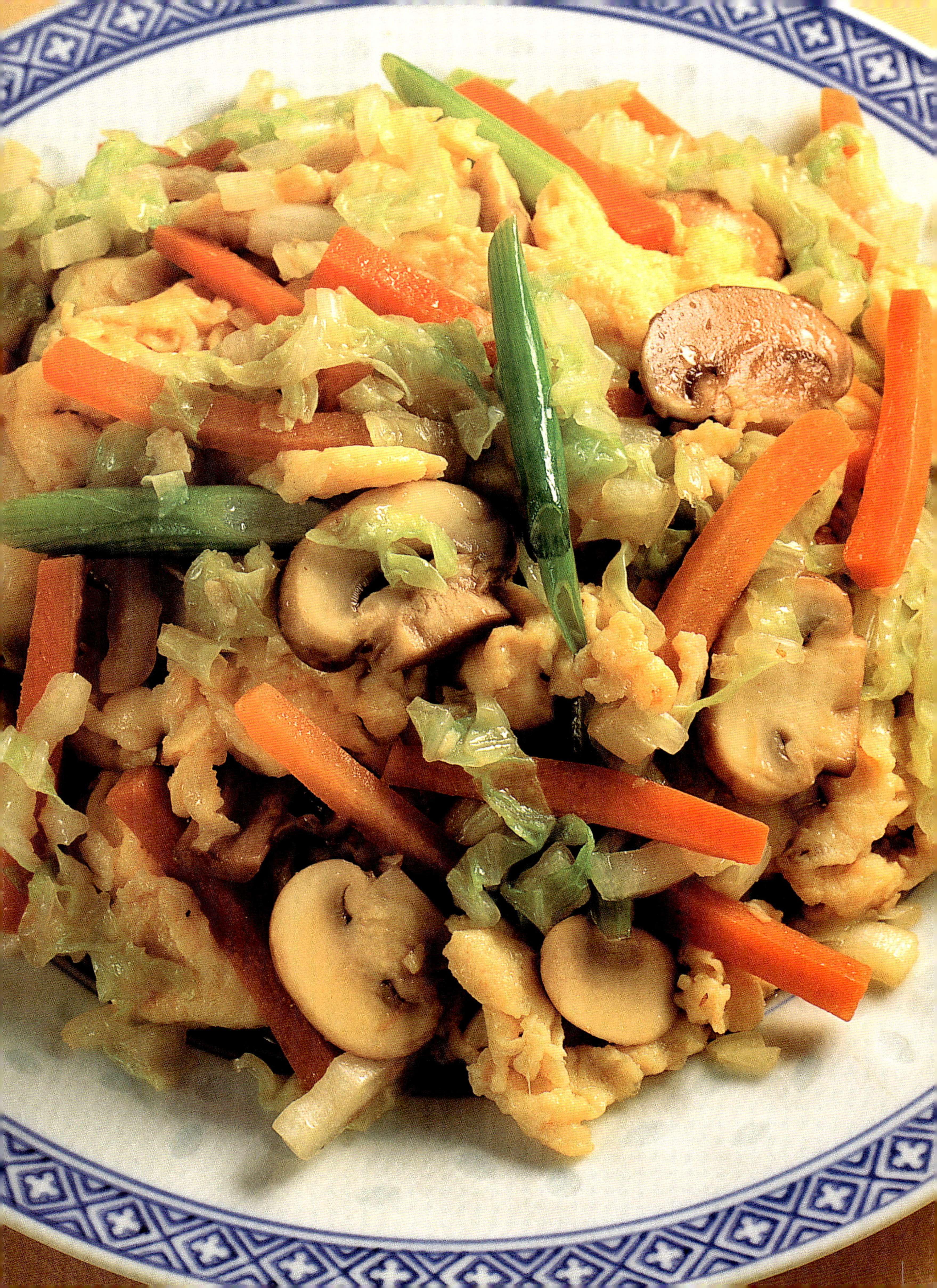

egg curry

serves 6

8 eggs
1 tablespoon oil
2 large onions, finely chopped
4 cloves garlic, finely chopped
1 tablespoon finely grated fresh ginger
1 tablespoon ground coriander
2 teaspoons ground cumin
1 teaspoon ground turmeric
½ teaspoon chilli powder
3 large ripe tomatoes, diced
salt to taste
1 teaspoon Garam Masala (see p. 4)

Hard-boil eggs and cool quickly in a bowl of cold water. Shell the eggs. Heat oil in a large, heavy frying pan and fry onions, garlic and ginger over low heat, stirring frequently, until golden brown. Add ground spices and fry for a few seconds. Add tomatoes and salt, cover and cook until tomatoes are pulpy. Stir in 240 ml (8 fl oz) hot water; cover and simmer until mixture is thickened. Add Garam Masala. Slice eggs in halves lengthwise and carefully stir into sauce. Heat through and serve with rice or chapatis.

parsi omelette

The Parsis fled Iran 1300 years ago. As Zoroastrians, a religious minority persecuted by the Moslems, they found sanctuary in India. Their cuisine is still influenced by Persia.

serves 2

- 1–2 potatoes, diced
- 2 tablespoons ghee or oil
- 4 eggs
- salt and pepper to taste
- ½ teaspoon ground cumin
- 2 tablespoons finely chopped fresh coriander
- 1 small onion, finely chopped
- 2 fresh green chillies, seeded and chopped

Parboil potato; drain well. Heat half of ghee or oil in a frying pan and fry potato until lightly browned. Beat egg whites until frothy. Add salt, pepper, cumin, coriander, onion and chillies. Heat remaining ghee or oil in an omelette pan, swirling to coat. Pour in egg mixture and when it starts to set, sprinkle fried potato on top. Cover over low heat, turning once until golden brown on both sides. Serve hot with flat Indian bread or readily available pita bread.

szechwan-style braised bean curd

It is important to buy firm bean curd, as soft bean curd will disintegrate with this style of cooking. If all you can get is soft bean curd, make the sauce and pour it over but don't try to fry the bean curd or simmer it for long.

serves 4

- 500 g (1 lb) block firm bean curd
- 60 ml (2 fl oz) peanut oil
- 1 tablespoon finely chopped garlic
- 3 teaspoons finely chopped fresh ginger
- 3 tablespoons hoi sin sauce
- 3 tablespoons bean sauce
- ½–1 teaspoon chilli bean sauce
- 1 teaspoon oriental sesame oil
- 1 teaspoon sugar
- 1 small red capsicum

After removing bean curd from plastic pouch, wrap in paper towels and press gently to remove excess moisture. The kind I buy is 10 cm (4 in) square and 5 cm (2 in) deep. Cut block into 32 cubes, each measuring 2.5 cm (1 in).

Reserve 1 tablespoon of peanut oil and heat remainder in a wok. Fry half the bean curd at a time until cubes are pale golden, drain on paper towels. Pour off remaining oil and clean wok with paper towels.

Heat reserved oil and on low heat fry garlic and ginger, stirring, until pale gold, about 2 minutes. If they start to brown remove from heat immediately and pour in rest of ingredients mixed with 120 ml (4 fl oz) water. Add bean curd and simmer, covered, for 10 minutes. Cut red capsicum into bite-sized squares and toss through bean curd for 1 minute, not long enough to diminish its crisp texture. Serve immediately with rice.

Note   I have also cooked this dish without deep frying the bean curd. While the bean curd is not as deeply golden, it is softer in texture.

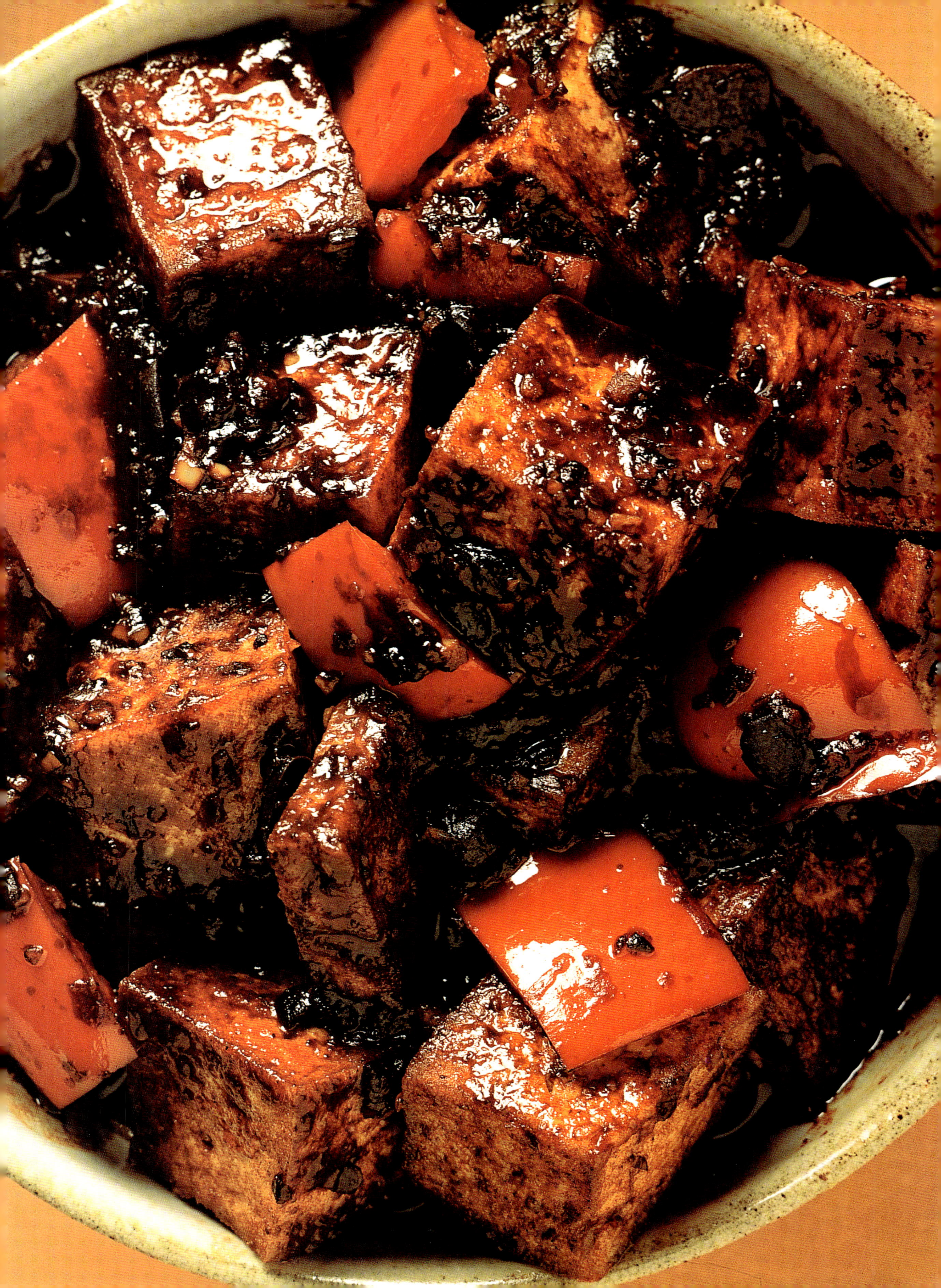

savoury tempeh mince

If your meat-eating friends try this recipe, they will find it hard to believe it is vegetarian.

serves 6

240 g (8 oz) tempeh
120 ml (4 fl oz) peanut oil
2 large onions, finely chopped
4 cloves garlic, finely chopped
2 teaspoons finely chopped fresh ginger

2 or 3 fresh chillies, sliced, or pickled hot chillies
1 tablespoon soy sauce
½ teaspoon ground black pepper
500 g (1 lb) potatoes
salt to taste

Let tempeh thaw at room temperature, then cut blocks into thin slices before dicing finely. Reserve a tablespoon of oil and heat remainder in a wok or small deep pan and when very hot fry half the tempeh at a time until golden brown. Lift out on perforated spoon and drain on paper towels. Pour off any remaining oil and heat wok with reserved oil. Fry onions, garlic, ginger and chillies over gentle heat, stirring frequently, until onions are translucent and start to brown. Add tempeh, soy sauce and pepper, turn off heat.

Peel and finely dice potatoes, drop into lightly salted boiling water, boil until soft, drain in colander. Mix into tempeh mixture, mashing potatoes slightly, and add salt to taste. Serve with rice.

Note Mixture may also be shaped into patties and shallow fried, first dipping into beaten egg, then breadcrumbs. Accompany with a salad of sliced tomato and cucumber.

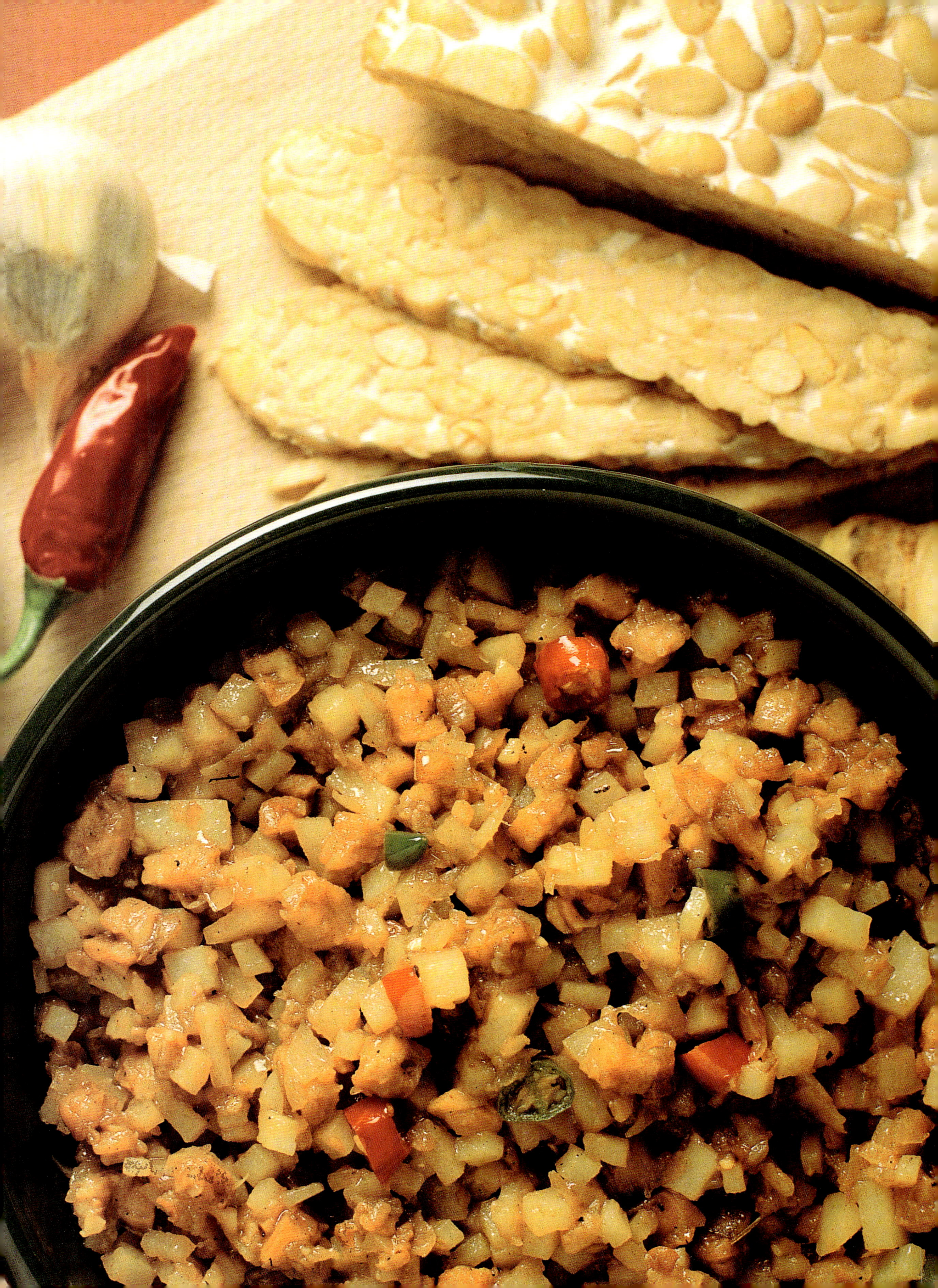

chick peas in spicy tomato sauce

serves 6

330 g (11 oz) dried chick peas
1 or 2 bay leaves
1 teaspoon ground turmeric
salt to taste
1 tablespoon oil
3 large onions, finely chopped
3 cloves garlic, chopped
1 tablespoon finely chopped fresh ginger

1½ teaspoons Garam Masala (see p. 4)
3 large ripe tomatoes, peeled and chopped
1 fresh green chilli, seeded and sliced
15 g (½ oz) chopped fresh mint leaves
salt to taste

Cover chick peas with cold water and soak overnight. Drain, rinse and place in a heavy saucepan with bay leaves and turmeric. Cover with water. Bring to boil, cover and simmer till almost tender. Add salt, cook until done. Drain, reserving liquid.

In a heavy pan heat oil and fry onion, garlic and ginger over low heat, stirring frequently, until golden. Add Garam Masala, tomatoes, chilli, drained chick peas and half the mint; stir well to mix. Add 120 ml (4 fl oz) reserved cooking liquid, cover and simmer, stirring occasionally, until peas are tender and tomatoes reduced to a purée. Add salt and sprinkle with remaining mint. Serve with chapatis or rice.

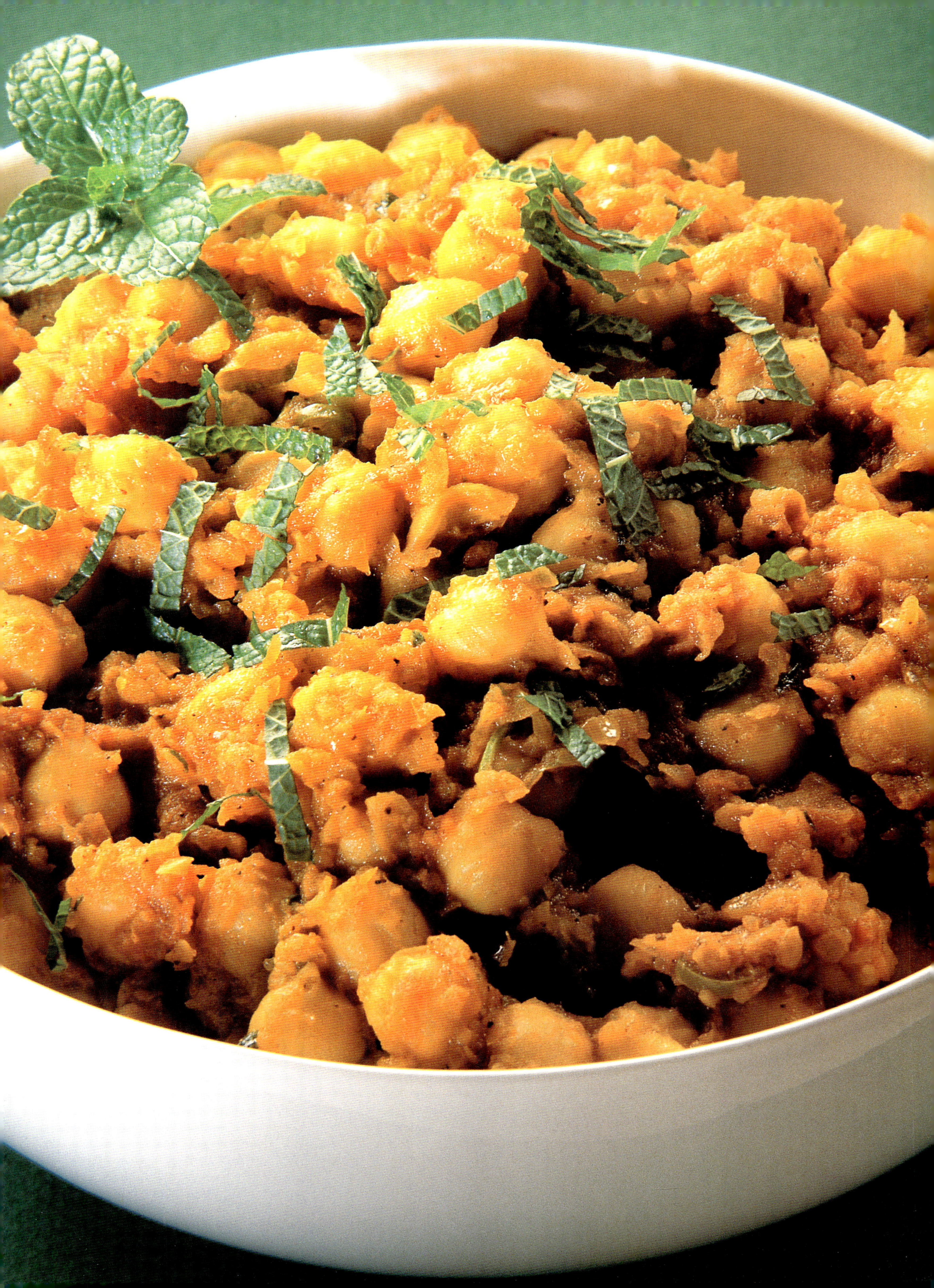

fresh cheese koftas in creamy sauce

Only home-made cheese (panir) is suitable for this recipe – cottage and ricotta cheese don't work.

serves 4

2 litres (64 fl oz) full cream milk
60 ml (2 fl oz) lemon juice
3 tablespoons finely chopped coriander leaves
2 tablespoons chopped sultanas
2 tablespoons chopped almonds
2 teaspoons chopped fresh chillies, optional
salt and pepper to taste
oil and ghee for deep-frying

sauce
1 tablespoon ghee or butter
2 teaspoons finely chopped garlic
1 onion, finely chopped
3 tablespoons tomato paste
1½ teaspoons salt
1 tablespoon sugar
1 tablespoon fine shreds of ginger
120 ml (4 fl oz) cream
1 teaspoon Garam Masala (see p. 4)
3 tablespoons chopped fresh coriander

Bring milk to the boil, stir in lemon juice, remove from heat and let stand for 15 minutes, then drain in muslin-lined colander. (Save the whey, you will be using it in the sauce.) Leave for 30 minutes. When as much moisture as possible has been removed, break curds into pieces and knead vigorously until smooth and palm of hand feels greasy. Divide into 8 equal portions and roll each into a ball.

Combine coriander, sultanas, almonds and chillies, adding salt and pepper to taste. Make a depression in each ball and fill with some of the coriander mixture, then mould ball around filling again, making a smooth surface without cracks. Heat about 600 ml (20 fl oz) oil with 60 ml (2 fl oz) ghee to flavour it and fry cheese koftas on medium heat until golden brown all over, then drain on paper towels.

Sauce

In a heavy pan melt ghee or butter and cook garlic and onion until soft and translucent. Add tomato paste, salt, sugar and ginger and stir in 360 ml (12 fl oz) whey. Cover and simmer for 10 minutes. Stir in cream. Simmer koftas in sauce for 10 minutes. Sprinkle with Garam Masala and coriander and serve with Indian bread or rice.

To make panir

Bring 1 litre (32 fl oz) milk to the boil, stirring occasionally. As it starts to boil, stir in 60 ml (2 fl oz) lemon juice. Remove from heat and leave 5 minutes. Curds will form. Strain through muslin, tie and let hang for at least half an hour. To remove as much moisture as possible, press between two plates with a weight on top.

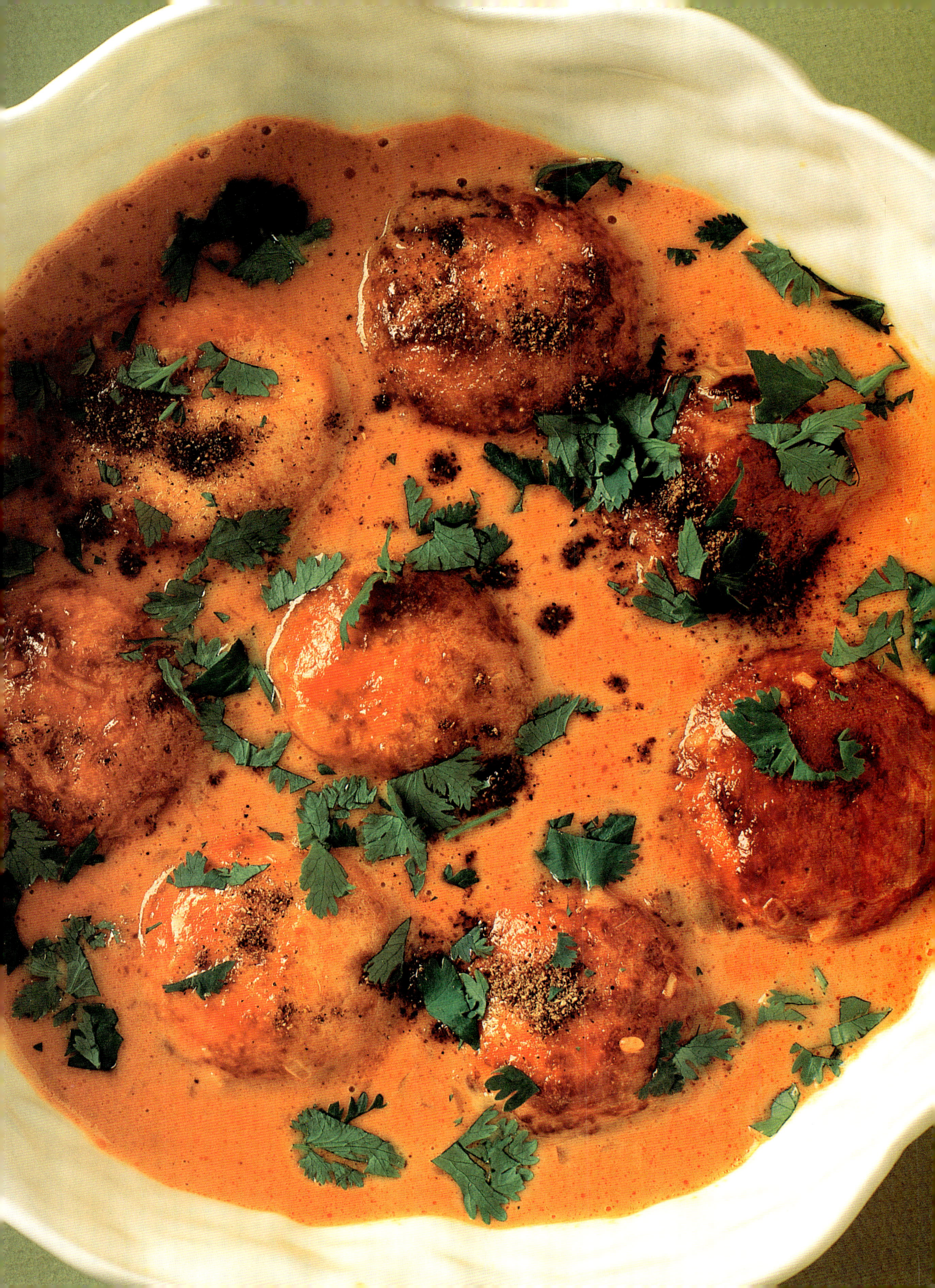

peas with fresh cheese

In India a fresh cheese known as panir is used for this dish. a good substitute is baked ricotta from Italian delicatessens. You can also make your own panir.

serves 6

- 360 g (12 oz) baked ricotta (see Note)
- 1 kg (2 lb) fresh peas in the pod or 750 g (1½ lb) frozen peas
- 2 tablespoons ghee or oil
- 1 large onion, finely chopped
- 3 teaspoons finely chopped garlic
- 3 teaspoons finely grated fresh ginger
- 1 tablespoon ground coriander
- 2 teaspoons ground cumin
- 1 teaspoon ground turmeric
- 1 teaspoon chilli powder, optional
- 3 ripe tomatoes, chopped or 270 g (9 oz) canned tomatoes
- 1 teaspoon salt or to taste
- 1½ teaspoons Garam Masala (see p. 4)
- 6 tablespoons finely chopped fresh mint or coriander

Cut ricotta into 2-cm (¾-in) dice. Shell peas or thaw frozen peas. Heat ghee or oil in a heavy saucepan and gently fry onion, garlic and ginger until soft, translucent and just turning golden. Add ground spices and stir for 1 minute, then add tomatoes, salt and 1 teaspoon Garam Masala. Stir, cover and cook until tomatoes can be easily mashed into a pulp. Add a little water if mixture sticks to pan. Add peas and cook until almost tender. Add cheese and half the fresh herbs and simmer, covered, for 10 minutes or until peas are tender. Sprinkle remaining Garam Masala over, stir well and serve with Indian bread.

Note For baked ricotta buy a 400–500 g (1 lb) block of ricotta and cut in halves. Wrap both halves in a clean linen tea towel and leave for 30 minutes so that excess moisture is absorbed. Place on a foil-lined baking tray and bake in a moderate oven for 20 minutes or until golden. Turn over with a frying slice and bake for a further 20 minutes. Leave to cool and cut into dice.

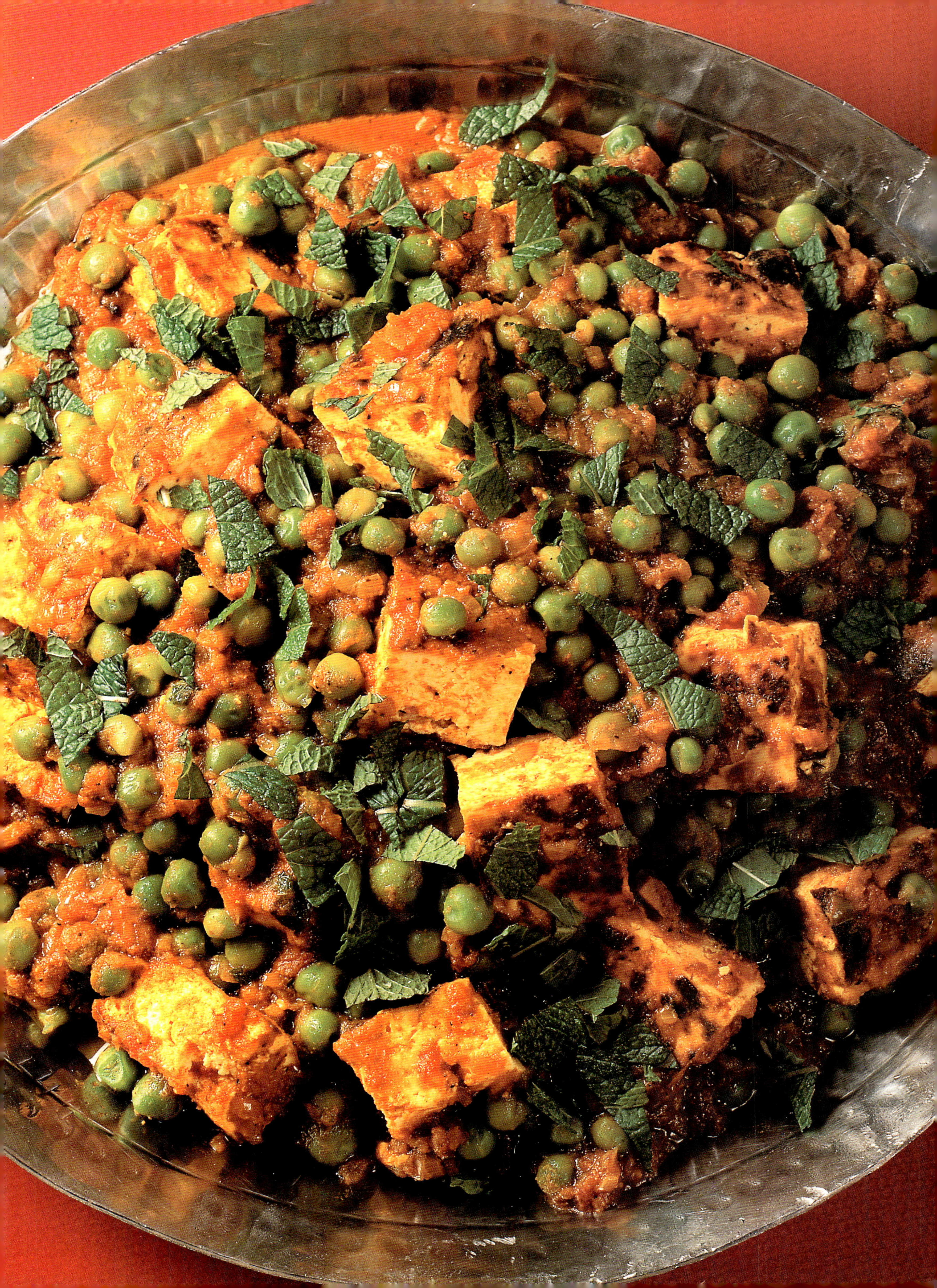

savoury kidney beans

serves 6

- 240 g (8 oz) red or brown kidney beans
- 1 onion stuck with 4 cloves
- 3 cardamom pods
- 1 teaspoon salt
- 2 tablespoons oil
- 1 tablespoon ghee, optional
- 2 onions, finely chopped
- 3 cloves garlic, finely chopped
- 2 teaspoons finely chopped fresh ginger
- 2 teaspoons ground cumin
- 1 teaspoon turmeric
- 180 g (6 oz) chopped ripe tomatoes or canned tomatoes
- ½ teaspoon Garam Masala (see p. 4)
- 3 tablespoons chopped fresh coriander

Soak beans in plenty of water overnight. Rinse, put into a saucepan with fresh water to cover, onion and cardamom pods. Bring to the boil, lower heat and simmer, covered, for 1 hour, then add salt and continue cooking until beans are very tender.

In another pan heat oil and ghee and cook chopped onions, garlic and ginger over low heat, stirring occasionally, until onions are very soft, translucent and starting to turn golden – about 20 minutes. Add cumin and turmeric and fry, stirring, for a few seconds, then add tomatoes and beans together with about 240 ml (8 fl oz) of their cooking liquid. Cover and simmer for 20 minutes, then sprinkle with Garam Masala and coriander and cook 5 minutes. Serve with rice or chapatis.

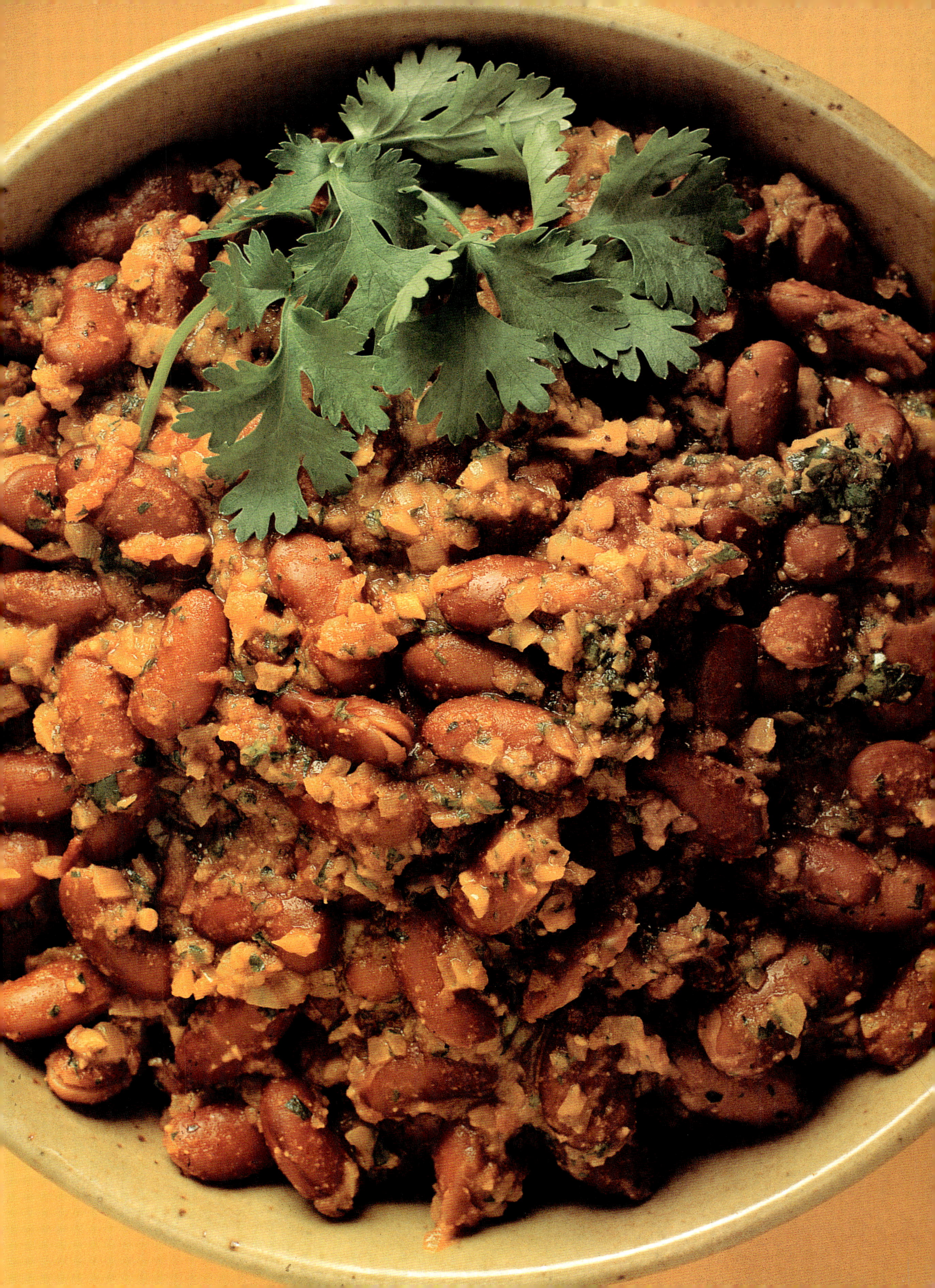

purée of red lentils

Rice and lentils are the staple foods of India and this simple but delicious lentil purée is served with rice and chapatis at least once a day. Other types of lentils may be used, but allow a longer cooking time.

serves 6

- 330 g (11 oz) red lentils
- 3 tablespoons ghee or oil
- 2 large onions, finely sliced
- 2 cloves garlic, crushed
- 2 teaspoons finely grated fresh ginger
- 1 teaspoon ground turmeric
- 2 teaspoons salt, or to taste
- 1 teaspoon Garam Masala (see p. 4)

Pick over lentils to remove any bits of grit. Wash in a bowl of cold water and drain well in colander. Heat ghee and fry onions over moderate heat until golden brown. Stir in garlic, ginger and turmeric, fry until garlic and ginger are golden.

Add lentils and fry for 2 minutes, stirring. Add 1.5 litres (60 fl oz) hot water, bring to the boil, then reduce heat and simmer, covered, for 15 minutes. Stir in salt and Garam Masala and continue cooking until lentils are soft and liquid has been absorbed. Serve with rice or Indian bread.

The recipes here are a little more highly spiced and intended to be taken in small quantities. Since most Asian meals are built around rice, and rice can be bland, it is understandable that chutneys, sambals and piquant relishes are important accompaniments to meals.

The chutneys featured here are fresh and not intended to be stored for long periods, as are the western adaptation of chutneys. Thanks to a certain Major Grey, who made a name (and probably a fortune) with his bottled jam-like creations, it is now hard to convince the world that the original chatni is made in minutes, eaten within a few hours and bears no resemblance to what one finds on the shelves of a western supermarket.

coconut and fresh herb chutney

serves 6

- 3 tablespoons desiccated coconut
- 60 g (2 oz) washed and chopped fresh coriander or mint leaves
- 6 tablespoons chopped spring onions
- 1 fresh green chilli, seeds removed
- 1 teaspoon sugar
- 1 teaspoon salt
- ½ teaspoon Garam Masala (see p. 4)
- 60 ml (2 fl oz) strained lemon juice

Sprinkle coconut with 3 tablespoons water and mix with fingertips to moisten. Put all ingredients in a blender and blend on high speed to a smooth purée. If necessary add a little water to help mixture over blades, but chutney should not be too wet.

Note For those who have access to fresh curry leaves, try this chutney using tender, young curry leaves (stripped from the centre rib). Grind them up with the coconut in place of mint or coriander. The flavour is quite unusual, but for most people it is love at first bite. Use fresh coconut too, if you can – it is milky and nicer than desiccated coconut.

tamarind chutney

A sweet-sour, very tangy fresh chutney made in a few minutes.

makes about 1 cup

- 3 tablespoons dried tamarind pulp
- 1 tablespoon brown or raw sugar
- 1 teaspoon ground cumin
- ½ teaspoon ground fennel
- ½ teaspoon finely grated fresh ginger
- lime or lemon juice to taste
- salt to taste

Place tamarind pulp in a bowl and cover with 240 ml (8 fl oz) hot water. Leave to soak until water cools. Squeeze pulp until it dissolves. Strain through a nylon sieve, pushing all the pulp through, and adding a little more water if necessary. Discard fibres and seeds. Add remaining ingredients and stir until well mixed. Leftover chutney will keep in refrigerator for 1 or 2 days.

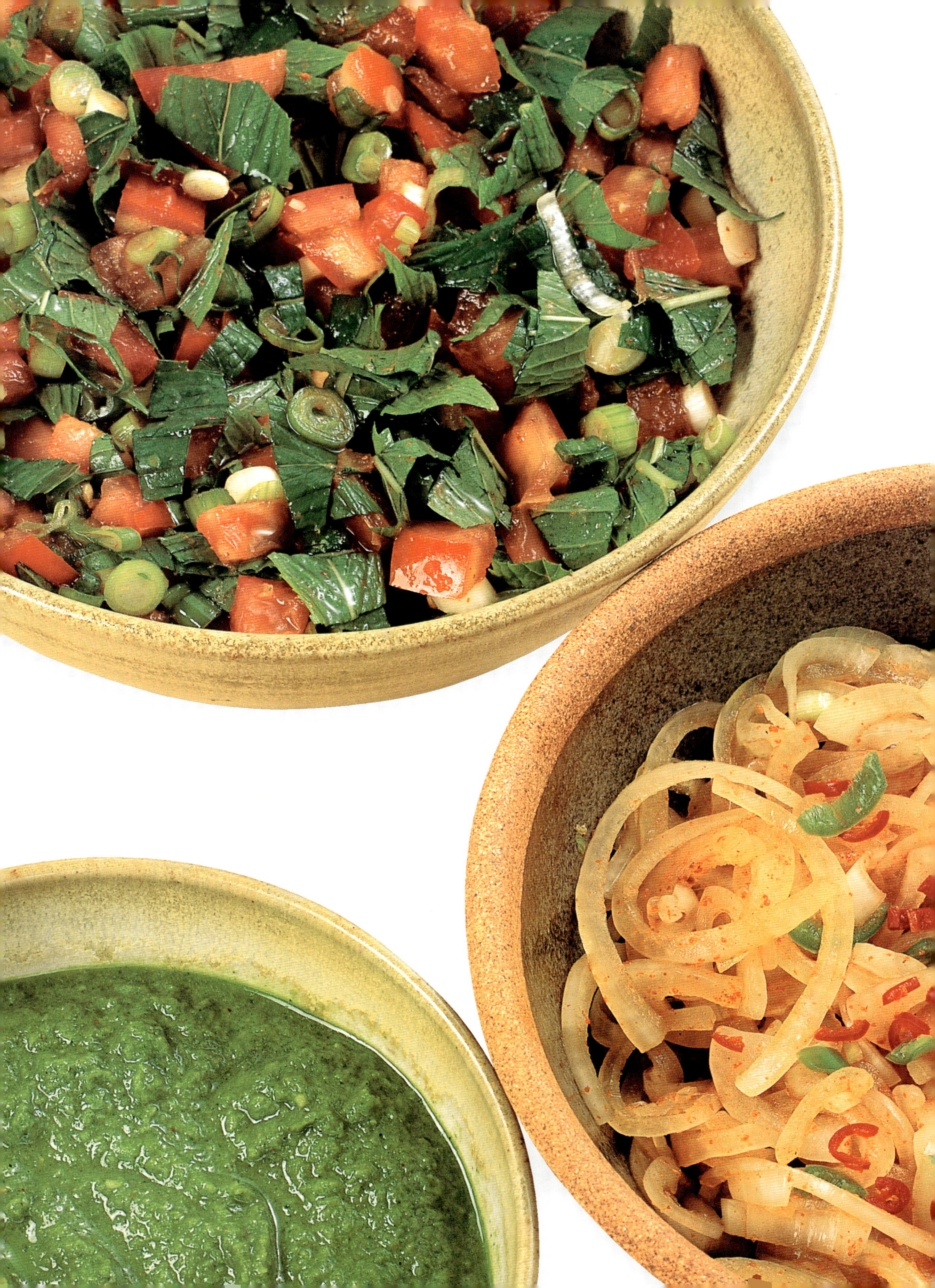

fried onion sambal

serves 6 to 8

- 4 large onions
- 120 ml (4 fl oz) oil
- 8 large red dried chillies
- 4 tablespoons lemon juice
- 1 teaspoon salt or to taste
- 2 tablespoons sugar

Peel onions and cut into thick slices. Heat oil and slowly fry onion until soft and turning golden brown. Snip chillies into pieces with scissors, shake out seeds and discard stems. Add to onions, cover and cook gently for a further 20 minutes or until deep brown but not burnt. Stir in lemon juice, salt and sugar. Serve with rice and curries.

onion, tomato and chilli salad

A typical salad served throughout India as an accompaniment to rice, curries and other main dishes

serves 6

- 2 medium onions
- salt
- 2 teaspoons dried tamarind pulp
- 2 tablespoons brown sugar
- 2 firm, ripe tomatoes
- 2 fresh red or green chillies, sliced
- 1 tablespoon finely shredded fresh ginger
- 2 tablespoons chopped fresh coriander leaves

Cut onions in halves lengthwise and then across into fine slices. Sprinkle with plenty of salt and set aside for 1 hour. Press out all liquid, rinse with cold water and drain well. Soak tamarind in 120 ml (4 fl oz) hot water until softened, squeeze to dissolve pulp and strain seeds and fibres. Add brown sugar to tamarind liquid and stir until dissolved. Scald tomatoes, peel and dice. Mix all ingredients, add salt if necessary, cover and chill until ready to serve.

pickled cabbage

One of Korea's national dishes, it is now possible to buy it in specialty Asian food stores and delicatessens. Ask for Kim Chi.

- 1 large white Chinese cabbage (wongah bok)
- common salt or sea salt (not iodised)
- cayenne pepper
- 6 spring onions, finely chopped
- 1 tablespoon finely chopped garlic
- 3 fresh red chillies, finely chopped
- 1 tablespoon finely chopped fresh ginger
- 500 ml (17 fl oz) dashi stock (see Note)
- 2 teaspoons light soy sauce

Cut base off cabbage and discard. Slice remainder lengthwise into 6 segments. Place on a tray and dry in sun for half a day. Cut each segment in halves crossways. Place in an earthenware pot alternately with good handfuls of salt and a sprinkling of cayenne pepper. Make several layers. Cover with a wooden board just small enough to fit inside pot so that it rests directly on the cabbage and weights it down. Leave for 1 week then rinse cabbage thoroughly under cold running water and squeeze out as much moisture as possible. Slice across into 2.5-cm (1-in) sections and return to the rinsed out pot, this time layering with a mixture of chopped spring onions, garlic, chillies and ginger. Mix dashi stock with soy sauce and fill pot. Cover with waxed paper; replace lid and refrigerate. The pickle will be ready to eat after 4 or 5 days. (In cold weather this pickle does not require refrigeration, but when the weather is warm store in refrigerator for up to 3 weeks.)

Note Make up stock according to instructions on packet or bottle of dashi concentrate.

ginger relish

Traditionally eaten as an after-meal digestive, this recipe from Burma also goes well with rice. Try and get young, pink-tipped ginger root, with almost transparent skin. Once the skin turns thick and gold it is too tough for this recipe.

makes about 1½ cups

- 120 g (4 oz) tender fresh ginger
- 6 tablespoons lemon juice
- 1 tablespoon peanut oil
- 1 tablespoon oriental sesame oil
- 4 cloves garlic, peeled and finely sliced
- 2 tablespoons sesame seeds
- salt to taste

Rub skin off ginger or scrape with a small, sharp knife. Slice finely, then cut into slivers. Pour lemon juice over and marinate for one hour, or until ginger turns pink. Heat oils in a wok and gently fry garlic over low heat until pale golden. Immediately remove and drain before it burns. Allow to cool and crisp. In a dry frying pan, roast sesame seeds over medium heat, stirring until golden brown. Turn onto a plate to cool. When ready to serve, drain ginger and put in a dish. Season with salt, sprinkle with fried garlic and sesame seeds and toss to combine.

glossary

You can find these ingredients in Asian stores, but many are also sold in supermarkets too.

Bean curd
Made from soy beans and high in protein, this is available fresh in various forms – soft, firm or fried. Soft bean curd has the consistency of junket. Firm bean curd (pressed bean curd) is sold in 400 g or 500 g (1 lb) blocks. It is easier to cook because it does not break up when stirred. Fried bean curd comes in golden brown cubes, creamy white and spongy inside. All types may be found in the refrigerator section of Asian stores. Fresh bean curd may be kept refrigerated for up to three days.

Cardamom
Strongly fragrant seed pods of a plant of the ginger family: there are two kinds – large black pods or small green pods. Use the latter, bruised slightly to release the fragrance. For ground cardamom, open the pods and pound the small brown or black seeds inside with a mortar and pestle.

Chilli bean sauce
Sold in jars, this is very hot and should be used with discretion.

Chillies
Handle with care as the volatile oils can cause discomfort to the eyes and skin. Wear gloves when handling. Buy chopped chillies in jars or sambal ulek, a mixture of fresh chillies and salt. Tabasco pepper sauce will also add zing. Soak dried chillies before using. Small chillies are hotter than large ones.

Cinnamon
Most of what is sold as cinnamon is really cassia, which is not as delicate. True cinnamon quills have many layers of fine, pale brown bark and, when ground, are pale beige rather than brown.

Cloves
The dried flower buds of a tropical tree, these can be overpowering, so don't use more than the stated amount.

Coconut milk
Some brands of canned coconut milk are very thick and rich, others are extremely thin. Mix the former with at least an equal amount of water; use the latter undiluted.

Coriander
Coriander seeds and fresh coriander are different in flavour and usage. Dried ground coriander seeds are one of the main ingredients in curries; fresh coriander herb is an essential ingredient in Thai and Chinese cooking.

Cumin
Sold as whole seeds or ground, this spice has a lemony fragrance and is a major component of curries.

Curry leaves (*Murraya koenigii*)
Available as fresh curry leaves or dried. You can also grow the plant itself.

Fennel seeds
Larger and lighter coloured than cumin, with a licorice flavour.

Fish sauce
A thin, salty sauce used in South East Asian food much as soy sauce is used in Far Eastern food.

Galangal (*Alpinia galanga*)
Two species of galangal – greater and lesser – are used in Asian food. Greater galangal is used throughout South East Asia. Outside Asia it is available in jars, in large white slices. It may also be purchased frozen, dried or powdered, the latter being known as laos powder.

Ghee
Clarified butter, sold in tins. Ghee can be heated to a high temperature without burning because it has no milk solids.

Ginger
Fresh rhizomes are usually available at any greengrocer. Dried ground ginger is no substitute in Asian cooking.

Hoi sin sauce
A thick, dark, sweet bean sauce.

Kalonji seeds (*Nigella*)
Sometimes called black cumin, although not a member of the cumin family. There is no substitute. Sold mostly in Indian shops.

Laos powder
See Galangal.

Lemon grass
Grows easily in tropical and temperate areas. Use the white or pale green portion of the stem, which is tender enough to slice finely. If fresh lemon grass is not available, rather than use the dried or powdered version, substitute two strips of thinly peeled lemon zest for each stem of lemon grass.

Mushrooms
Dried Chinese or Japanese mushrooms are the shiitake variety. Dried European mushrooms are no substitute.

Okra
A furry green pod, very popular in India. Buy only tender ones, if mature they are impossibly stringy.

Oyster sauce
A thick sauce used in Chinese food.

Palm sugar
Obtained from various tropical palms, it has a distinct flavour, but you may substitute brown sugar for it.

Saffron
Try to get true saffron because there are many imitations and nothing else has the same flavour. Expensive, but very little is needed and it keeps well if stored airtight. It is sold in strands (best to buy these) or tiny packets of powder. There is no such thing as cheap saffron.

Sambal ulek (*oelek*)
See Chillies.

Sesame oil
Use oriental sesame oil made from roasted sesame, which is dark in colour and very aromatic. Light coloured sesame oil (usually sold in health food stores) will not impart the same flavour.

Shrimp paste
Made from dried shrimp, this is used in tiny quantities and is a mainstay of South East Asian cuisines. Sold in jars or blocks. Keeps indefinitely.

Soy sauce
For the best results, use the type specified in the recipe.

Star anise
A dried, star-shaped seed pod that imparts flavour to Chinese food. Simmered in long-cooked dishes.

Tamarind
Gives acidity to many dishes. It is sold dried, puréed or instant. The dried pulp has the truest flavour.

Turmeric
A tropical rhizome, it is most readily available as a yellow powder used to flavour and colour food.

Wasabi
Green horseradish powder, it is always served (in minute amounts) with raw fish dishes such as sashimi and sushi.

Water chestnuts
Available in cans. After opening, store in water in the refrigerator for a week, changing water daily.

Yoghurt
The best yoghurt to use is natural yoghurt, not the skim milk variety, which seems to have a greater acidity and overpowers other flavours.

index

bean curd, Szechwan-style braised 72
beans, savoury kidney 82
   stir-fried snake, and cashews 10
braised bok choy 32
   vegetable combination 58
broccoli with peanut sauce 28

cabbage in coconut milk 34
   pickled 89
carrot and relish salad 52
carrots, piquant 50
cashews, stir-fried snake beans and 10
cauliflower and green masala 29
cauliflower, steamed 36
cheese, fresh, koftas in creamy sauce 78
   fresh, peas with 80
chick peas, eggplant purée with 60
   in spicy tomato sauce 76
chilli and leeks 38
   tomato, onion and, salad 88
   banana, stuffed and braised 14
Chinese-style eggplant 18
chutney, coconut and fresh herb 86
   tamarind 86
coconut and fresh herb chutney 86
   milk, cabbage in 34
   pumpkin in 26
coconut, mixed vegetables with 66
cooked green salad 41
   steamed potatoes 44
creamy eggplant relish 20
   sauce, cheese koftas in 78
curry, cucumber or ridged gourd 16
   egg 70
   pea pods 4
   pineapple 24
   yam 48

dry-fry okra 12
   zucchini or squash 22

egg curry 70
stir-fried, with vegetables 68
eggplant, Chinese-style 18
   purée with chick peas 60
   relish 20

fresh cheese koftas in creamy sauce 78
   peas with 80
fresh herb, coconut and, chutney 86
fried onion sambal 88
fritters, dried vegetable 56

gado gado 64
garam masala 4
ginger relish 89
green masala paste 29
green peas in coconut milk 8

kidney beans, savoury 82

leeks and chilli 38
lentils, purée of red 84

mixed vegetables with spinach 30
   with coconut 66

okra, dry-fried 12
omelette, Parsi 71
onion, tomato and chilli salad 88

pakorhas 56
Parsi omelette 71
pastries, potato and pea 49
pea pods, curried 4
peanut sauce 64
peas, green, in coconut milk 8
   potato and, pastries 49
   snap, Thai-style stir-fried 6
   with fresh cheese 80
pepper and coriander paste 28
pickled cabbage 89
pineapple curry 24
piquant carrots 50
potato and pea pastries 49
potatoes, steamed 44
   sweet-sour 46
pumpkin in coconut milk 26
purée, eggplant, with chick peas 60
   red lentils 84

radish, carrot and, salad 52
relish, creamy eggplant 20
   ginger 89
ridged gourd curry 16

salad, carrot and radish 52
   cooked green 41
   onion, tomato and chilli 88
sambal, fried onion 88
savoury kidney beans 82
   tempeh mince 74
snap peas, Thai-style stir-fried 6
spiced mixed vegetables 62
spicy tomato sauce, chick peas in 76
spinach with mixed vegetables 30
squash dry-fry 22
steamed cauliflower 36
stir-fried eggs with vegetables 68
   snake beans and cashews 10
stuffed and braised banana chillies 14
sweet-sour potatoes 46
Szechwan-style braised bean curd 72

tamarind chutney 86
Thai-style stir-fried snap peas 6
tomato, onion and chilli salad 88

vegetarian savoury mince 74
vegetable combination, braised 58
   fritters 56
   spiced mixed 62
   stir-fried eggs with 68
   with peanut sauce 64

water convolvulus in sweet gravy 40

yam curry 48

zucchini dry-fry 22